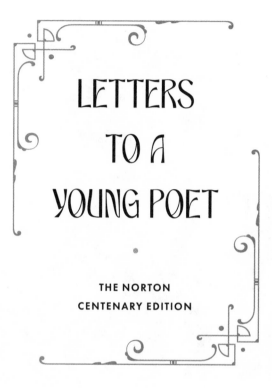

LETTERS
TO A
YOUNG POET

THE NORTON
CENTENARY EDITION

Rainer Maria Rilke (1875–1926),
Austrian writer born in Prague, photograph 1925
SMITH ARCHIVE / ALAMY STOCK PHOTO

LETTERS TO A YOUNG POET

Rainer Maria Rilke

Translated by
M. D. HERTER NORTON

THE NORTON CENTENARY EDITION

Foreword by Damion Searls
Afterword by Julia A. Reidhead

W. W. NORTON & COMPANY
Celebrating a Century of Independent Publishing

For information about permission to reproduce selections from this book,
write to Permissions, W. W. Norton & Company, Inc.,
500 Fifth Avenue, New York, NY 10110

For information about special discounts for bulk purchases, please contact
W. W. Norton Special Sales at specialsales@wwnorton.com or 800-233-4830

Manufacturing by Lakeside Book Company
Book design by Beth Steidle
Production manager: Lauren Abbate

ISBN 978-1-324-05072-8

W. W. Norton & Company, Inc., 500 Fifth Avenue, New York, N.Y. 10110
www.wwnorton.com

W. W. Norton & Company Ltd., 15 Carlisle Street, London W1D 3BS

1 2 3 4 5 6 7 8 9 0

CONTENTS

M. D. Herter Norton
PHOTOGRAPH COURTESY OF ALEXIA NORTON JONES

FOREWORD

never made the connection either: that M. D. Herter Norton, translator of the classic versions of Rilke published by Norton, was in fact the same Norton. The storied publishing house was and is, of course, "W. W. Norton & Company," but William Warder was MDH's husband and they'd founded the press together, on a beach in Nantucket. I am not alone in failing to get it—it's been news to everyone I've told over the years since someone told me. In a fan letter addressed "Dear Sirs" and mailed to W. W. Norton & Company in January 1939, a good ten years after Virginia Woolf "venture[d] to guess that Anon was often a woman," one Grover Jacoby Jr., from Los Angeles, wrote, "I think Mr. Norton is especially to be praised" for his virtuosic yet modest Rilke translations, and closed with a "hope that you and Mr. Norton will continue the good work."

She and Mr. Norton did.

IN HER AFTERWORD TO THIS BOOK, JULIA REIDHEAD DIS-
cusses Mrs. Mary Norton (1894–1985), co-founder,
universally known to her friends, her admiring employees,
and later generations of beneficiaries of her great generosity
as "Polly." She describes Polly's youth as a progressive child
of privilege—studying violin in Europe and at Juilliard,
helping out in her father's pioneering at-home fourth-floor
medical laboratory in their town house at 819 Madison
Avenue, horseback riding in Central Park, enjoying Sun-
day afternoon recitals on the pipe organ that had been
built into the house's ground floor—and how the values
of that upbringing would shape the publishing house she
built. In this foreword, I would like to talk less about Polly
or Mrs. Norton than about MDH, the underappreciated
writer, translator, musicologist, and artist.

Especially important perhaps: educator. The fact about
the publishing house most crucial throughout MDH's
career was that it had grown out of adult education. WW,
unfulfilled as head of the Export Department of Irwin,
Harrisons & Crosfield, Ltd., had a deep interest in social
work—he was treasurer of the American Association
of Social Workers in the early 1920s—and was actively
working with Cooper Union on adult education under the
rubric The People's Institute. According to Polly, WW's
initial idea was to print those lectures in order to make
them more widely available as extension courses: thus was
born the People's Institute Publishing Company. Their

early efforts were cardboard box sets of twenty different lecture-pamphlets, and after bookstores complained
about stocking them (customers would walk off with one
or two, or leave them out of order), the lectures were soon
bound into books; by 1926, with their expanded catalog of
publications, the People's Institute Publishing Company
had changed its name to the less limiting W. W. Norton & Company. It would go on to be probably the most
important college publisher in America, with its Norton Anthologies and Norton Critical Editions, and what
made this success possible, in large part, was that by the
time of the GI Bill and postwar education boom, the firm
had decades of experience and infrastructure behind it,
including a well-developed college marketing team. That
background is what set Norton apart from all the other
major publishers founded just prior (Knopf in 1915, Har-
court Brace in 1920) or soon afterward (Viking, Simon &
Schuster, Random House).

In 1925, MDH published her own book, *String Quartet
Playing: A New Treatise on Chamber Music*, and dedicated it
to the members of the Kneisel Quartet, the leading string
quartet in America, three of whom had been her teach-
ers; Franz Kneisel himself—one of the leading classical
violinists in America, the first head of the violin department of the new Juilliard School of Music (then called the
Institute of Musical Art), and a renowned and demanding
teacher—reviewed and endorsed the manuscript. It was

while studying under Louis Svećenski, the violist and only other original member of the Kneisel Quartet to play in it during its whole thirty-two-year history, that MDH got the idea for the book. Her pedagogical bent is clear: she covers who should sit where and what kind of music stands to use, how loud *forte* actually is, and so on, up to bigger and fancier problems. Even decades later, in 1962, when a revised edition came out under the title *The Art of String Quartet Playing: Practice, Technique, and Interpretation*, Isaac Stern would write in his introduction, "It is really surprising to find that [this] book is the only one available for competent direction to the *player* (as opposed to the listener) of string quartets."

MDH's first translation that I have been able to find grew out of her interest in music and musicology: a co-translation with Alice Kortschak of Paul Bekker's *The Story of Music*, itself a collection of, in effect, adult education lectures. As Bekker put it in his foreword: "The Southwest German Radio Corporation asked me if I were prepared to give a series of lectures in the Radio High School on the history of music. . . . As a self-taught individual, I felt some scruple about trusting myself in a matter which seemed to demand treatment by a professional historian of music. On the other hand, I had to admit that the present academic attitude toward music history is scarcely calculated to bring the subject nearer to the layman."

After 1950, while she continued to translate such surveys

as Walter Wiora's *The Four Ages of Music* (1965) and Friedrich Blume's *Classic and Romantic Music: A Comprehensive Survey* (1972) and *Renaissance and Baroque Music: A Comprehensive Survey* (1975), along with shorter musicological pieces such as Thomas Mann's "Letter to Bruno Walter on His Seventieth Birthday" for the *Musical Quarterly* in 1946, her family connections expanded her range: she is credited with "helping to edit" her second husband Daniel Crena de Iongh's touristic 1967 book *Byzantine Aspects of Italy*, and she translated history books by Jane de Iongh, *Margaret of Austria, Regent of the Netherlands* and *Mary of Hungary: Second Regent of the Netherlands*. But it was the middle period of her career that produced the works she is most remembered for outside the field of music: her translations of Rilke.

MDH IS ONE OF THE HANDFUL OF PEOPLE WHO CAN CLAIM to have done more for Rilke's global reputation than anyone in the world, along with Rilke's German publisher and perhaps Franz Xaver Kappus, who kept Rilke's letters to him and decided to publish them after Rilke's death as the *Letters to a Young Poet*. There had been scattered English translations of his work before his death in late 1926, but soon afterward Leonard and Virginia Woolf's Hogarth Press emerged as Rilke's major English-language publisher: Rilke was one of Leonard's favorite poets, and for a time Insel Verlag in Germany granted Hogarth the exclusive rights to publish Rilke's poetry. Hogarth published the first English translation of the *Duino Elegies*, by Vita and her cousin Edward Sackville-West, in 1931 (about which more below), and the first truly extensive selections of his poetry translated by J. B. Leishman: *Poems* (1934), *Requiem and Other Poems* (1935), *Sonnets to Orpheus* (1936), and *Later Poems* (1938).

Norton in America, meanwhile, tackled the prose. Elling Aannestad, the firm's first assistant in 1927 and later an editor and major presence in the company, had read Rilke; he knew the Woolfs and the Hogarth Press, and he brought Rilke to WW and MDH's attention, as he later would bring Freud. MDH wrote, "It was Elling who liked the *Cornet* and encouraged Warder to publish Rilke." They published the first translation of Rilke's only novel in 1930, acquired from Hogarth—as *Journal of My Other Self*, in a translation credited to a Scottish minister named John Linton together with MDH, while the Hogarth edition, credited only to Linton, bore the title suggested by Leonard Woolf that would become standard: *The Notebook of Malte Laurids Brigge* (usually later called "Notebooks"). In 1932, MDH published translations of two more short prose works, *Stories of God* (credited to her and Nora Purtscher-Wydenbruck, whose earlier version she heavily revised) and *The Tale of the Love and Death of Cornet Christopher Rilke*. And in 1934 came her edition of *Letters to a Young Poet*.

In retrospect the decision to publish this slim collection of ten letters written in Rilke's twenties was obvious, and extremely profitable, selling well over a million copies in the next seventy-five years. But at the time it required unique insight, as shown by an amazing document in her granddaughter's possession.* While Norton and other American publishers turned down Leishman's *Poems* and *Requiem*, Leonard Woolf rejected *Letters to a Young Poet* for Hogarth, writing to WW on March 21, 1935, that while he found Mrs. Norton's translations "extraordinarily good," the text itself was "too slight" for Hogarth to "do anything with" it in Europe.

MDH had published three previous books of Rilke's prose, of course, but Norton's educational focus surely helped her see the value of the *Letters to a Young Poet* as a guide to life for what would prove to be millions of readers. She also offered a further education of her own. A long biographical note at the end of the book, conceived and written by MDH, served to truly introduce Rilke to American audiences, and would for the first decade or so be almost as much remarked on by readers and critics as the text itself. Here, too, Aannestad made an impor-

---

* I would like to take this moment to thank Alexia Norton Jones, not only for the trove of fascinating material that vastly deepened my understanding of her grandmother, but for being an eager and helpful source of anecdote and information for me and, I know, for the others writing pieces in celebration of W. W. Norton's centenary.

tant contribution, writing in a letter to MDH, "I hope you can call your 'Biographical Note' something else, something more inviting, such as 'Chronicle.' I wouldn't want anyone to miss what you've written there, and they might—I wouldn't blame them—skip 'B. N.' They are excellently done. (Selecting just what material you would use must have been difficult.) But tantalizing, too; one wants more." Here, too, Leonard Woolf's instincts proved weak: the other reason he gave for rejecting her edition for Hogarth, besides slightness, was that they were about to publish a collection of Rilke's poetry with an introduction covering much of the material in the Chronicle, and they were reluctant to "repeat the same thing in another book." MDH's substantial, thirty-page Chronicle has much of the rhythm and pacing of a full biography; Leishman's biographical introduction was soon forgotten.

It is a bit misleading to say that Hogarth concentrated on the poetry while Norton concentrated on the prose, certainly after the 1934 *Letters to a Young Poet*. MDH would publish *Translations from the Poetry of Rainer Maria Rilke* in 1938 and *Sonnets to Orpheus* in 1942; perhaps more important, she would steer Hogarth towards its new translation of the *Duino Elegies* (1939). That said, MDH's other three Rilke translations were all of his letters—*Wartime Letters* in 1940, and *Selected Letters*, volumes I and II, with Jane Bannard Greene, in 1945 and 1948: still in print and still the main translation of his letters into English. Her version of *Letters to a Young Poet*, meanwhile, has continued as the standard for more than three-quarters of a century. When I was asked to retranslate the book for Norton, I reread the earlier translations and found hers the best one to date.

Which came as another surprise to me, because today MDH's reputation as a translator is not especially high. The quality of her translations has been unappreciated largely, I think, because of how she described herself: she took up the cudgels for faithfully following the original and providing "the closest idiomatic parallel" for it, which often put her in a straw-man position compared to other translators. Once she drew the distinction, in her 1938 introduction to *Translations from the Poetry of Rainer Maria Rilke*, between a poem's "intrinsic qualities" of content and image, and the "technical elements of form," i.e., rhyme and meter, and stated her goal of prioritizing the former, she all but invited accusations of being blind to the poem's language.

A 1975 paper at the Rilke Centennial conference by Ingo Seidler, published in 1980 and purporting to give an overview of Rilke translations into English, is partial and rather slanted but typical for the time, shortly before Stephen Mitchell's 1982 *Selected Poetry of Rainer Maria Rilke* would reshape the landscape of Rilke translations. Seidler defines a continuum of translators' approaches, with "Mrs. Herter Norton's faithful transliterations" (ouch) on one end and "Robert Lowell's dashing 'imitations'" (dashing!) on the other. Lowell then gets two and a half pages and several close readings, while Norton's work is dismissed in half a paragraph:

> *This language altogether lacks the sensuous appeal of Rilke's; neither his technical brilliance nor his richness, neither his music nor his magic, are here preserved. No one would therefore wish to call these renditions poems. . . . To call these translations "literary trots" or "prose cribs" would be a trifle ungenerous; they are too carefully worked and too sensitively balanced. Even so, living poems they are not.*

Just a *trifle* ungenerous!

As is so often the case when someone is alleged to take an utterly unreasonable position, that position was actually adopted in the context of a different debate. Hogarth had published *Duineser Elegien: Elegies from the Castle at Duino*, translated by the Woolfs' friends the Sackville-Wests, in 1931. It was lambasted, then and for the next ninety years. Paulina Choh's useful essay on Rilke in the Modernist Archives Publishing Project,[*] from which I have taken many other historical details for this foreword, describes it this way:

---

[*] www.modernistarchives.com/person/rainer-maria-rilke

As a limited edition, artisanal printing with a price point to match, it was an anomaly among the Hogarth Press' hand-printed or commercially printed books. The Woolfs had not been involved in the design or printing and bore no financial responsibility; its distribution under the Press was considered a personal courtesy to the Sackville-Wests. The poor quality of the Sackville-West translation was widely criticized by scholars of Rilke, leading the Woolfs to select an academic to translate their future publications of Rilke, processes in which Leonard would be highly involved.

That academic was J. B. Leishman, whose many translations won favor at the time for systematically preserving all of Rilke's meters and rhymes, even alternating masculine and feminine rhyme schemes—at the cost, needless to say, of countless extraneous or omitted words and phrases, empty and also likewise purposeless filler, word orders unidiomatic, and oft-ludicrous compounds and neologistic thesaurus-ransacking. In one case Leishman uses "deciduous," in a rhyme with "thus," for the normal and monosyllabic German word for "tree."

As I write this, the Sackville-Wests' reviled *Duino Elegies* has recently found its own champions: Pushkin Press reissued it in 2021 with an introduction by Lesley Chamberlain pointing to its "evident quality." The Sackville-Wests put the *Elegies* entirely into blank verse, resulting in some (though far less) Leishmaniacal padding or trimming without the excuse of copying other features of the original. As Chamberlain points out, though, blank verse is "the most traditional and versatile" English meter, and the Sackville-Wests were thus able to make their English "immediately intelligible and gripping." When I read this translation today, it doesn't sound like the Rilke I know, but it does sound like good solid traditional poetry:

> For beauty's nothing but the birth of terror,
> Which we endure but barely, and, enduring,
> Must wonder at it, in that it disdains
> To compass our destruction. Every angel
> Is terrible, and thus in self-control
> I crush the appeal that rises with my sobs.

There is certainly a strong case to be made that their version sounds more like poetry than Leishman's efforts. Poetry from fifty years before the publication date, perhaps, but English poetry nonetheless.

These dueling visions of Rilke don't really fit on Seidler's "continuum" from Herter Norton to Lowell. (Seidler unhelpfully puts Leishman "somewhere in between" the two, even though Leishman's slavishness to Rilke's rhyme and meter arguably makes him far more devoted to "faithfulness" over "beauty" than MDH, and he neglects the Sackville-Wests altogether, calling Leishman and Spender's 1939 *Duino Elegies* the oldest version in English.) The relevant distinction at the time was really between literary amateurs and academic professionals. Leonard Woolf caved to the predominantly academic English critics and cast his lot with the professionals; MDH, as one would have expected from Paul Bekker and everything else in her career, took the other side. I haven't found any explicit mention she makes of the Sackville-Wests' Rilke, but she did turn down Leishman's *Poems* and *Requiem*, and Norton refused to publish Leishman's *Duino Elegies* unless Stephen Spender was involved. Spender was a successful poet himself, and he and Leishman quarreled over the former's preference for exact meaning and imagery, in loose or irregular meter (unlike the Sackville-Wests), while Leishman argued it was more important to keep the rhyme and meter than match the content, but in the end they came together and Hogarth published their *Duino Elegies* in 1939. In this context, MDH arguing for "the closest idiomatic parallel" for a poem's "intrinsic qualities" of content and image was of a piece with insisting that Spender co-translate the *Duino Elegies*, against Leishman's credentials. It certainly wasn't advocating for "literary trots" or "prose cribs."

The fact is that even if MDH thought of herself as sticking to the German, she couldn't have produced "sensitively balanced," much less superbly readable, English if she actually had stuck to the German. In a memo to WW explaining her revisions of Nora Purtscher-Wydenbruck's earlier version of *Stories of God*, MDH described what she was doing as "using Rilke's own words and adhering to the rhythm of his prose," but that is misleading: she used English words and rhythm, and changed what needed changing. Changing "God created the Earth" to "God made the Earth," for "*machte*," isn't using Rilke's own words, or even matching the number of syllables—it's just better writing in English. Elsewhere in the memo she wrote: "As you know, I have always believed that a simple, very close adherence to the original most justly conveys the quality of Rilke's style, and that his German and our English language are not so unrelated as to make this impossible." Yet her previous sentence called for "simple words, clarity, and typical rhythm"—not mentioning something her work proves she knew, namely that simplicity, clarity, and typicality are different in different languages.

Even more revealing than comparing her published work to other translators' are her draft revisions, revisions of others' work, and notes on others' suggestions to her, all material available in her granddaughter's family archive. These documents are full of MDH switching tenses, swapping verbs and nouns, nouns and adjectives ("difficult sorrow" to "difficulty and sadness")—diverging whenever necessary in the interest of clarity and rhythm. In response to a suggested revision to *Cornet*: "We cannot use an infinitive because the German does." In a draft of *Letters to a Young Poet*, where the draft had said "not out of physical suffering, bending to necessities," a handwritten note: "does it need 'but'? —not in the German." The final translation follows the needs of English, not the German: "not out of physical suffering, but bending to necessities." What we really see her doing in these revisions is listening to English, not "adhering to" German: she attends to sentence or line rhythms, melodious and forceful language, words and word order that stay truest to Rilke's "music."

I said MDH's were the best translations to date, and that would certainly be true if the English language itself hadn't changed. Later versions of *Letters to a Young Poet* were needed, and some are arguably more readable now, through no fault of her own—it is the language itself in her version that seems, while not archaic, a bit old-fashioned. Take the famous passage in the first letter's first paragraph, one of the great excuses in history for not giving honest feedback on someone's bad poetry:

> *With nothing can one approach a work of art so little as with critical words: they always come down to more or less happy misunderstandings. Things are not all so comprehensible and expressible as one would mostly have us believe; most events are inexpressible, taking place in a realm which no word has ever entered, and more inexpressible than all else are works of art, mys-*

terious existences, the life of which, while ours passes away, endures.

The roundabout construction of the first sentence—"With nothing so little as with"—is difficult and a bit off-putting today; we rarely use the impersonal pronoun "one" anymore (I didn't just write "one rarely uses . . ."), and MDH uses it twice here. We wouldn't say "all else" nowadays, we'd say "everything else." These are road bumps to reading that time, not the translator, has created in English.

Aside from them, though, MDH's translation is very good. It is tight and short—almost every passage of her version set alongside other versions has fewer words and takes up less space. Her handling of the last clause here, while again a bit roundabout ("the life of which, while"), has a stately iambic grandeur, ending with the powerful, positive, stressed "endures." By way of comparison, my own version untangles the word order while also putting "endures" in a strong prominent position and using the rhythm of the sentence to suggest the conceptual contrast between the two forms of life, but it is not as monumental: "works of art: those mysterious creatures whose life endures, alongside our own life, which is so fleeting."

What sets MDH's *Letters to a Young Poet* apart is this stately grandeur. Every translator is "faithful," but to something different: to whatever he or she feels is most important to preserve. To some extent, what's most important to preserve in a given translation depends on the publishing context: Is it an academic monograph, a textbook for language learners, a popular trade book with no footnotes? More fundamentally, though, it depends on what the translator finds in the original—how the translator *reads*. Every translator practices what MDH called "very close adherence to the original," but they are working from different originals—trying to produce a text that matches, or does the same as, not the source text but *his or her reading of the source text*. That is why there is no objectively "best" translation, one that is "closest" to "the" original, as MDH's formulation falsely implies there is. Each translator translates a different thing, in precisely the same way that each reader of a given book is reading a different book (and yet, in another way, not). In judging a translator, the ideal of "faithfulness" is an empty tautology: we are really judging what they see in the author or text and choose to be faithful to. At least in the case of good translators. Some bad translators simply can't re-create what they find—can't make their jokes funny, can't set the lyrical parts singing, or simply misunderstand what the book says—but I think such failures are relatively few.

Ultimately, MDH's work, more than just being concise or having "better" rhythm or word choice, is defined by her vision of who Rilke is. For her, he is the canonical Great Man, one who speaks to us all—whose works belong on an adult education syllabus, as it were. Her Translator's

Note, the first page of text in her edition, frames Rilke as follows: "It is evident that a great artist, whatever the immediate conditions disturbing his own life, may be able to clarify for the benefit of another those fundamental truths the conviction of which lies too deep in his consciousness to be reached by external agitations." In general, the fact that Rilke wrote his letters of advice and consolation in his twenties doesn't mean for MDH that they were immature, for his mature great spirit was always speaking through him: throughout his life "the legend of the weary poet is dispelled, and in the end we find him always young, always constructive, the eminently positive philosopher of these letters." Her version of the sentence I quoted above, about how the artwork endures, is more monumental than mine because her Rilke is more monumental than mine; what I see when I read is a Rilke who's a bit more approachable, listening, in dialogue with the young poet.

Naturally MDH would offer a Chronicle of Rilke's life in which the poet moves from precocious strength to anticipated future glory. Of course she would translate and publish Rilke's *Wartime Letters* from the World War I years in 1940, while Leonard Woolf at Hogarth was reluctant to work with a German publisher under the Nazi regime at all (Choh: "Unconvinced by Leishman's arguments that the artistic and cultural value of Rilke's works transcended political and moral concerns, Leonard considered boycotting collaboration and went so far as to write Leishman in an attempt to be released from the contract"); numerous letters in her granddaughter's archive praise and thank MDH for standing up for timeless artistic values and reminding the world in 1940 that not all Germans were like the Nazis. It is not surprising that she left herself and her own views entirely out of her introductions, afterwords, and notes—nowhere revealing even the fact that "M. D." was a woman.

Rilke as M. D. Herter Norton read and translated him is an important and vital one to have in English—stately and capacious, with dignity and authority—and her diligent, devoted, artistic work on the melody and music of his writing made it come alive for her generation of readers, and for ours.

DAMION SEARLS

LETTERS
TO A
YOUNG POET

TRANSLATOR'S NOTE

How these letters came to be written is told by their recipient in his introduction, and to this there would be nothing to add were it not for the close of the eighth letter: "Do not believe that he who seeks to comfort you lives untroubled among the simple and quiet words that sometimes do you good. His life has much difficulty and sadness. . . . Were it otherwise he would never have been able to find those words." It is evident that a great artist, whatever the immediate conditions disturbing his own life, may be able to clarify for the benefit of another those fundamental truths the conviction of which lies too deep in his consciousness to be reached by external agitations. Though Rilke expresses himself with a wisdom and a kindness that seem to reflect the calm of self-possession, his spirit may have been speaking out of its own need rather than from the security of ends achieved, so that his words indeed reflect desire rather than fulfillment. In what sort this was the case becomes apparent on perusal of the several volumes of his correspondence. From these, for the most part, the accompanying chronicle of the years 1903–1908 has been prepared. It shows what Rilke was going through in his own relationship to life and work at the period in question (he turned twenty-eight in December 1903). Perhaps such a record may in a measure explain, too, why sympathy was always so responsive an element of his nature. Certainly—despite low physical vitality that often reduced him to actual ill-health, despite lack of funds and homeless wandering in search of the right places and circumstances for his work, despite all the subjective fret and hindrance because of which some think to see in him a morbidly conditioned fantasy—the legend of the weary poet is dispelled, and in the end we find him always young, always constructive, the eminently positive philosopher of these letters.

M. D. HERTER NORTON
New York, October 1934

INTRODUCTION

I t was in the late autumn of 1902—I was sitting under some ancient chestnuts in the park of the Military Academy in Wiener-Neustadt, reading. So deeply was I absorbed in my book, I scarcely noticed when the only civilian among our professors, the Academy's learned and kindly Parson Horaček, came to join me. He took the volume from my hand, contemplated the cover, and shook his head. "Poems of Rainer Maria Rilke?" he asked reflectively. He then turned the pages here and there, skimmed a couple of verses, gazed thoughtfully into the distance, and finally nodded. "So our pupil René Rilke has become a poet."

And I learned of the thin, pale boy, whom his parents had sent more than fifteen years ago to the Lower Military School at Sankt-Pölten so that he might later become an officer. Horaček had been chaplain to that institution at the time, and he still remembered his former student perfectly. He described him as a quiet, serious, highly endowed boy who liked to keep to himself, patiently endured the compulsions of boarding-school life and after his fourth year moved on with the others into the Military College, which was situated at Mährisch-Weisskirchen. Here indeed it became apparent that his constitution could not stand the strain, for which reason his parents removed him from the school and let him continue his studies at home in Prague. How the course of his life had since shaped itself Horaček could not say.

After all this it is not hard to understand how I determined in that very hour to send my poetic attempts to Rainer Maria Rilke and to ask him for his opinion. Not yet twenty, and close on the threshold of a profession which I felt to be entirely contrary to my inclinations, I hoped to find understanding, if in anyone, in the poet who had written *Mir zur Feier*. And without having intended to do so at all, I found myself writing a covering letter in which I unreservedly laid bare my heart as never before and never since to any second human being.

Many weeks passed before a reply came. The blue-sealed letter bore the postmark of Paris, weighed heavy in the hand, and showed on the envelope the same beautiful, clear, sure characters in which the text was set down from the first line to the last. With it began my regular correspondence with Rainer Maria Rilke which lasted until 1908 and then gradually petered out because life drove me off into those very regions from which the poet's warm, tender, and touching concern had sought to keep me.

But that is not important. Only the ten letters are important that follow here, important for an understanding of the world in which Rainer Maria Rilke lived and worked, and important too for many growing and evolving spirits of today and tomorrow. And where a great and unique man speaks, small men should keep silence.

FRANZ XAVER KAPPUS

Berlin, June 1929

THE

LETTERS

ONE

Paris, February 17th, 1903

My dear sir,

Your letter only reached me a few days ago. I want to thank you for its great and kind confidence. I can hardly do more. I cannot go into the nature of your verses; for all critical intention is too far from me. With nothing can one approach a work of art so little as with critical words: they always come down to more or less happy misunderstandings. Things are not all so comprehensible and expressible as one would mostly have us believe; most events are inexpressible, taking place in a realm which no word has ever entered, and more inexpressible than all else are works of art, mysterious existences, the life of which, while ours passes away, endures.

After these prefatory remarks, let me only tell you further that your verses have no individual style, although they do show quiet and hidden beginnings of something personal. I feel this most clearly in the last poem, "My Soul." There something of your own wants to come through to word and melody. And in the lovely poem "To Leopardi" there does perhaps grow up a sort of kinship with that great solitary man. Nevertheless the poems are not yet anything on their own account, nothing independent, even the last and the one to Leopardi. Your kind letter, which accompanied them, does not fail to make clear to me various shortcomings which I felt in reading your verses without however being able specifically to name them.

You ask whether your verses are good. You ask me. You have asked others before. You send them to magazines. You compare them with other poems, and you are disturbed when certain editors reject your efforts. Now (since you have allowed me to advise you) I beg you to give up all that. You are looking outward, and that above all you should not do now. Nobody can counsel and help you, nobody. There is only one single way. Go into yourself. Search for the reason that bids you write; find out whether it is spreading out its roots in the deepest places of your heart, acknowledge to yourself whether you would have to die if it were denied you to write. This above all—ask yourself in the stillest hour of your night: must I write? Delve into yourself for a deep answer. And if this should be affirmative, if you may meet this earnest question with a strong and simple "I must," then build your life according to this necessity; your life even into its most indifferent and slightest hour must be a sign of this urge and a testimony to it. Then draw near to Nature. Then try, like some first human being, to say what you see and experience and love and lose. Do not write love-poems; avoid at first those forms that are too facile and commonplace: they are the most difficult, for it takes a great, fully matured power to give something of your own where good and even excellent traditions come to mind in quantity. Therefore save yourself from these general themes and seek those which your own everyday life offers you; describe your sorrows and desires, passing thoughts and the belief in some sort of beauty—describe all these with loving, quiet, humble sincerity, and use, to express yourself, the things in your environment, the images from your dreams, and the objects of your memory. If your daily life seems poor, do not blame it; blame yourself, tell yourself that you are not poet enough to call forth its riches; for to the creator there is no poverty and no poor indifferent place. And even if you were in some prison the walls of which let none of the sounds of the world come to your senses— would you not then still have your childhood, that precious, kingly possession, that treasure-house of memories? Turn your attention thither. Try to raise the submerged sensations of that ample past; your personality will grow more firm, your solitude will widen and will become a dusky dwelling past which the noise of others goes by far away.— And if out of this turning inward, out of this absorption into your own world *verses* come, then it will not occur to you to ask anyone whether they are good verses. Nor will you try to interest magazines in your poems: for you will see in them your fond natural posses-sion, a fragment and a voice of your life. A work of art is good if it has sprung from necessity. In this nature of its origin lies the judgment of it: there is no other. Therefore, my dear sir, I know no advice for you save this: to go into yourself and test the deeps in which your life takes rise; at its source you will find the answer to the question whether you must create. Accept it, just as it sounds, without inquiring into it. Perhaps it will turn out that you are called to be an artist. Then take that destiny upon yourself and bear it, its burden and its greatness, without ever asking what recompense might come from outside. For the creator must be a world for himself and find everything in himself and in Nature to whom he has attached himself.

But perhaps after this descent into yourself and into your inner solitude you will have to give up becoming a poet; (it is enough, as I have said, to feel that one could live without writing: then one must not attempt it at all). But even then this inward searching which I ask of you will not have been in vain. Your life will in any case find its own ways thence, and that they may be good, rich and wide I wish you more than I can say.

What more shall I say to you? Everything seems to me to have its just emphasis; and after all I do only want to advise you to keep growing quietly and seriously throughout your whole development; you cannot disturb it more rudely than by looking out-ward and expecting from outside replies to questions that only your inmost feeling in your most hushed hour can perhaps answer.

It was a pleasure to me to find in your letter the name of Professor Horaček; I keep for that lovable and learned man a great veneration and a gratitude that endures through the years. Will you, please, tell him how I feel; it is very good of him still to think of me, and I know how to appreciate it.

The verses which you kindly entrusted to me I am returning at the same time. And I thank you once more for your great and sincere confidence, of which I have tried, through this honest answer given to the best of my knowledge, to make myself a little worthier than, as a stranger, I really am.

Yours faithfully and with all sympathy:
RAINER MARIA RILKE

TWO

Viareggio, near Pisa (Italy),
April 5th, 1903

You must forgive me, my dear sir, for only today gratefully remembering your letter of February 24th: I have been unwell all this time, not exactly ill, but oppressed by an influenza-like lassitude that has made me incapable of anything. And finally, as I simply did not get better, I came to this southerly sea, the beneficence of which has helped me once before. But I am not yet well, writing comes hard to me, and so you must take these few lines for more.

Of course you must know that every letter of yours will always give me pleasure, and only bear with the answer which will perhaps often leave you empty-handed; for at bottom, and just in the deepest and most important things, we are unutterably alone, and for one person to be able to advise or even help another, a lot must happen, a lot must go well, a whole constellation of things must come right in order once to succeed.

Today I wanted to tell you just two things more:

Irony: do not let yourself be governed by it, especially not in uncreative moments. In creative moments try to make use of it as one more means of grasping life. Cleanly used, it too is clean, and one need not be ashamed of it; and if you feel you are getting too familiar with it, if you fear this growing intimacy with it, then turn to great and serious objects, before which it becomes small and helpless. Seek the depth of things: thither irony never descends—and when you come thus close to the edge of greatness, test out at the same time whether this ironic attitude springs from a necessity of your nature. For under the influence of serious things either it will fall from you (if it is something fortuitous), or else it will (if it really innately belongs to you) strengthen into a stern instrument and take its place in the series of tools with which you will have to shape your art.

And the second point about which I wanted to tell you today is this:

Of all my books just a few are indispensable to me, and two even are always among my things, wherever

I am. They are about me here too: the Bible, and the books of the great Danish writer, Jens Peter Jacobsen. I wonder whether you know his works. You can easily get them, for some of them have come out in very good translation in Reclam's Universal Library. Get yourself the little volume of *Six Stories* of J. P. Jacobsen and his novel *Niels Lyhne*, and start on the first story in the former, called "Mogens." A world will come over you, the happiness, the abundance, the incomprehensible immensity of a world. Live a while in these books, learn from them what seems to you worth learning, but above all love them. This love will be repaid you a thousand and a thousand times, and however your life may turn,—it will, I am certain of it, run through the fabric of your growth as one of the most important threads among all the threads of your experiences, disappointments and joys.

If I am to say from whom I have learned something about the nature of creative work, about its depth and everlastingness, there are but two names I can mention: that of Jacobsen, the great, great writer, and that of Auguste Rodin, the sculptor, who has not his equal among all artists living today.

And all success upon your ways!

Yours:

RAINER MARIA RILKE

THREE

Viareggio, near Pisa (Italy),
April 23rd, 1903

You gave me much joy, my dear sir, with your Easter letter; for it said many good things about yourself, and the way you spoke of Jacobsen's great and beloved art showed me that I had not erred in guiding your life and its many questions to this source of plenty.

Now *Niels Lyhne* will open up before you, a book of glories and of the deeps; the oftener one reads it—there seems to be everything in it from life's very faintest fragrance to the full big taste of its heaviest fruits. There is nothing that does not seem to have been understood, grasped, experienced, and recognized in the tremulous after-ring of memory; no experience has been too slight, and the least incident unfolds like a destiny, and fate itself is like a wonderful, wide web in which each thread is guided by an infinitely tender hand and laid alongside another and held and borne up by a hundred others. You will experience the great happiness of reading this book for the first time, and will go through its countless surprises as in a new dream. But I can tell you that later too one goes through these books again and again with the same astonishment and that they lose none of the wonderful power and surrender none of the fabulousness with which they overwhelm one at a first reading.

One just comes to relish them increasingly, to be always more grateful, and somehow better and simpler in one's contemplating, deeper in one's belief in life, and in living happier and bigger. And later you must read the wonderful book of the destiny and desire of *Marie Grubbe* and Jacobsen's letters and pages from his diary and fragments and finally his poems, which (even if they are only fairly well translated) live in everlasting sound. (For this purpose I would advise you to buy when you have a chance the beautiful complete edition of Jacobsen's works which contains all these. It appeared in three volumes, well translated, brought out by Eugen Diederichs in Leipzig, and costs, I believe, only 5 or 6 marks a volume.)

In your opinion of "There should have been roses . . ." (that work of such incomparable delicacy and form) you are of course quite, quite unassailably right as against the writer of the introduction. And let me here promptly make a request: read as little as possible of aesthetic criticism—such things are either partisan views, petrified and grown senseless in their lifeless induration, or they are clever quibblings in which today one view wins and tomorrow the opposite. Works of art are of an infinite loneliness and with nothing so little to be reached as with criticism. Only love can grasp and hold and be just toward them. Consider yourself and your feeling right every time with regard to every such argumentation, discussion or introduction; if you are wrong after all, the natural growth of your inner life will lead you slowly and with time to other insights. Leave to your opinions their own quiet undisturbed development, which, like all progress, must come from deep within and cannot be pressed or hurried by anything. Everything is gestation and then bringing forth. To let each impression and each germ of a feeling come to completion wholly in itself, in the dark, in the inexpressible, the unconscious, beyond the reach of one's own intelligence, and await with deep humility and patience the birth-hour of a new clarity:

that alone is living the artist's life: in understanding as in creating.

There is here no measuring with time, no year matters, and ten years are nothing. Being an artist means, not reckoning and counting, but ripening like the tree which does not force its sap and stands confident in the storms of spring without the fear that after them may come no summer. It does come. But it comes only to the patient, who are there as though eternity lay before them, so unconcernedly still and wide. I learn it daily, learn it with pain to which I am grateful: patience is everything!

Richard Dehmel: His books affect me (and, incidentally, so does the man, whom I know casually) in such a manner that when I have found one of his beautiful pages I am always afraid of the next, which may upset everything again and turn what is attractive into something unworthy. You characterized him very well with the term: "living and writing in heat."— And in fact artistic experience lies so incredibly close to that of sex, to its pain and its ecstasy, that the two manifestations are indeed but different forms of one and the same yearning and delight. And if instead of heat one might say— sex, sex in the great, broad, clean sense, free of any insinuation of ecclesiastical error, then his art would be very grand and infinitely important. His poetic power is great, strong as a primitive instinct; it has its own unyielding rhythms in itself and breaks out of him as out of mountains.

But it seems that this power is not always honest and without pose. (But this again is one of the hardest tests of the creative individual: he must always remain unconscious, unsuspecting of his best virtues, if he would not rob them of their ingenuousness and untouchedness!) And then, where, as it rushes through his being, it comes to the sexual, it finds not quite so pure a man as it might require. Here is no thoroughly mature and clean sex world, but one that is not sufficiently *human*, that is only *male*, is heat, intoxication and restlessness, and laden with the old prejudices and arrogances with which man has disfigured and burdened love. Because he loves as man only, not as human being, for this reason there is in his sexual feeling something narrow, seeming wild, spiteful, time-bound, uneternal, that diminishes his art and makes it ambiguous and doubtful. It is not immaculate, it is marked by time and by passion, and little of it will survive and endure. (But most art is like that!) Nevertheless one may deeply rejoice in what there is of greatness in it, only one must not lose oneself in it and become an adherent of that Dehmelian world which is so unspeakably apprehensive, full of adultery and confusion, and so far from the real destinies that cause more suffering than these temporal afflictions but also give more opportunity for greatness and more courage for eternity.

Finally, as to my books, I would like best to send you all that might give you pleasure. But I am very poor, and my books, when once they have appeared, no longer belong to me. I cannot buy them myself—and, as I would so often like, give them to those who would be kind to them.

So I am writing you on a slip the titles (and publishers) of my most recent books (the latest, in all I believe I have published some 12 or 13) and must leave it to you, dear sir, to order some of them when occasion offers.

I like to think of my books as in your possession. Farewell.

Yours:

RAINER MARIA RILKE

FOUR

Worpswede, near Bremen,
July 16th, 1903

Some ten days ago I left Paris, quite ill and tired,
and journeyed into a great northerly plain whose
breadth and stillness and sky are to make me well
again. But I came into a long spell of rain that today
for the first time shows signs of clearing a little over
the restlessly wind-blown land; and I am using this
first moment of brightness to greet you, dear sir.

Very dear Mr. Kappus: I have left a letter from
you long unanswered, not that I had forgotten it—
on the contrary: it was of the sort that one reads
again, when one finds them among one's correspondence, and I recognized you in it as though you had
been close at hand. It was the letter of May 2nd, and

you surely remember it. When I read it, as now, in
the great quiet of these distances, I am touched by
your beautiful concern about life, more even than I
had felt it in Paris, where everything resounds and
dies away differently because of the too great noise
that makes things vibrate. Here, where an immense
country lies about me, over which the winds pass
coming from the seas, here I feel that no human
being anywhere can answer for you those questions
and feelings that deep within them have a life of
their own; for even the best err in words when they
are meant to mean most delicate and almost inexpressible things. But I believe nevertheless that you
will not have to remain without a solution if you will
hold to objects that are similar to those from which
my eyes now draw refreshment. If you will cling to
Nature, to the simple in Nature, to the little things
that hardly anyone sees, and that can so unexpect-
edly become big and beyond measuring; if you have
this love of inconsiderable things and seek quite
simply, as one who serves, to win the confidence of
what seems poor: then everything will become easier, more coherent and somehow more conciliatory
for you, not in your intellect, perhaps, which lags
marveling behind, but in your inmost consciousness, waking and cognizance. You are so young, so
before all beginning, and I want to beg you, as much

as I can, dear sir, to be patient toward all that is unsolved in your heart and to try to love the questions themselves like locked rooms and like books that are written in a very foreign tongue. Do not now seek the answers, which cannot be given you because you would not be able to live them. And the point is, to live everything. Live the questions now. Perhaps you will then gradually, without noticing it, live along some distant day into the answer. Perhaps you do carry within yourself the possibility of shaping and forming as a particularly happy and pure way of living; train yourself to it—but take whatever comes with great trust, and if only it comes out of your own will, out of some need of your inmost being, take it upon yourself and hate nothing. Sex is difficult; yes. But they are difficult things with which we have been charged; almost everything serious is difficult, and everything is serious. If you only recognize this and manage, out of yourself, out of your own nature and ways, out of your own experience and childhood and strength to achieve a relation to sex wholly your own (not influenced by convention and custom), then you need no longer be afraid of losing yourself and becoming unworthy of your best possession.

Physical pleasure is a sensual experience no different from pure seeing or the pure sensation with which a fine fruit fills the tongue; it is a great unending experience, which is given us, a knowing of the world, the fullness and the glory of all knowing. And not our acceptance of it is bad; the bad thing is that most people misuse and squander this experience and apply it as a stimulant at the tired spots of their lives and as a distraction instead of a rallying toward exalted moments. Men have made even eating into something else: want on the one hand, superfluity upon the other, have dimmed the distinctness of this need, and all the deep, simple necessities in which life renews itself have become similarly dulled. But the individual can clarify them for himself and live them clearly (and if not the individual, who is too dependent, then at least the solitary man). He can remember that all beauty in animals and plants is a quiet enduring form of love and longing, and he can see animals, as he sees plants, patiently and willingly uniting and increasing and growing, not out of physical delight, not out of physical suffering, but bowing to necessities that are greater than pleasure and pain and more powerful than will and withstanding. O that man might take this secret, of which the world is full even to its littlest things, more humbly to himself and bear it, endure it, more seriously and feel how terribly difficult it is, instead of taking it lightly. That he might be more reverent toward his fruitfulness, which is but one, whether it seems mental or physical; for intellectual creation too springs from the physical, is of one nature with it and only like a gentler, more ecstatic and more everlasting repetition of physical delight. "The thought of being creator, of procreating, of making" is nothing without its continuous great confirmation and realization in the world, nothing without the thousandfold concordance from things and animals—and enjoyment of it is so indescribably beautiful and rich only because it is full of inherited memories of the begetting and the bearing of millions. In one creative thought a thousand forgotten nights of love revive, filling it with sublimity and exaltation. And those who come together in the night and are entwined in rocking delight do an earnest work and gather sweetnesses, gather depth and strength for the song of some coming poet, who will arise to speak of ecstasies beyond telling. And they call up the future; and though they err and embrace blindly, the future comes all the same, a new human being rises up, and on the ground of that chance which here seems consummated, awakes the law by which a resistant vigorous seed forces its way through to the egg-cell that moves open toward it. Do not be bewildered by the surfaces; in the depths all becomes law. And those who live the secret wrong and badly (and they are very many), lose it only for themselves and still hand it on, like a sealed letter, without knowing it. And do not be confused by the multiplicity of names and the complexity of cases. Perhaps over all there is a great motherhood, as a common longing. The beauty of the virgin, a being that (as you so beautifully say) "has not yet achieved anything," is motherhood that begins to sense itself and to prepare, anxious and yearning. And the mother's beauty is ministering motherhood, and in the old woman there is a great remembering. And even in the man there is motherhood, it seems to me, physical and spiritual; his procreating is also a kind of giving birth, and giving birth it is when he creates out of inmost fullness. And perhaps the sexes are more related than we think, and the great renewal of the world will perhaps consist in this, that man and maid, freed of all false feelings and reluctances, will seek each other not as opposites, but as brother and sister, as neighbors, and will come together as human beings, in order simply, seriously, and patiently to bear in common the difficult sex that has been laid upon them.

But everything that may some day be possible to many the solitary man can now prepare and build with his hands, that err less. Therefore, dear sir, love your solitude and bear with sweet-sounding lamentation the suffering it causes you. For those who are near you are far, you say, and that shows it is beginning to grow wide about you. And when what is near you is far, then your distance is already among the stars and very large; rejoice in your growth, in which you naturally can take no one with you, and be kind to those who remain behind, and be sure and calm before them and do not torment them with your doubts and do not frighten them with your confidence or joy, which they could not understand. Seek yourself some sort of simple and loyal community with them, which need not necessarily change as you yourself become different and again different; love in them life in an unfamiliar form and be considerate of aging people, who fear that being-alone in which you trust. Avoid contributing material to the drama that is always stretched taut between parents and children; it uses up much of the children's energy and consumes the love of their elders, which is effective and warming even if it does not comprehend. Ask no advice from them and count upon no understanding; but believe in a love that is being stored up for you like an inheritance and trust that in this love there is a strength and a blessing, out beyond which you do not have to step in order to go very far!

It is good that you are presently entering a profession that will make you independent and set you entirely on your own in every sense. Wait patiently to find out whether your inner life feels cramped by the form of this profession. I consider it very difficult and very exacting, as it is burdened with great conventions and scarcely leaves room for a personal conception of its problems. But your solitude will be a hold and home for you even amid very unfamiliar conditions and from there you will find all your ways. All my wishes are ready to accompany you, and my confidence is with you.

Yours:

RAINER MARIA RILKE

FIVE

Rome, October 29th, 1903

My dear sir,

I received your letter of August 29th in Florence, and not till now—two months later—am I telling you of it. Forgive this dilatoriness—but I do not like writing letters while traveling, because I need more for letter-writing than the most necessary implements: some quiet and solitude and a not too incidental hour.

We arrived in Rome about six weeks ago, at a time when it was still the empty, hot, fever-discredited Rome, and this circumstance, together with other practical difficulties in getting settled, helped to make it seem that the unrest around us would not cease and the foreignness lay with the weight of homelessness upon us. Add to this that Rome (if one does not yet know it) has an oppressingly sad effect for the first few days: through the lifeless and doleful museum atmosphere it exhales, through the abundance of its pasts, fetched-forth and laboriously upheld pasts (on which a small present subsists), through the immense overestimation, sustained by savants and philologists and copied by the average traveler in Italy, of all these disfigured and dilapidated things, which at bottom are after all no more than chance remains of another time and of a life that is not and must not be ours. Finally, after weeks of being daily on the defensive, one finds oneself again, if still somewhat confused, and one says to oneself: no, there is not more beauty here than elsewhere, and all these objects, continuously admired by generations and patched and mended by workmen's hands, signify nothing, are nothing, and have no heart and no value;—but there is much beauty here, because there is much beauty everywhere. Waters unendingly full of life move along the old aqueducts into the great city and dance in the many squares over white stone basins and spread out in wide spacious pools and murmur by day and lift up their murmuring to the night that is large and starry here and soft with winds. And gardens are here,

unforgettable avenues and flights of stairs, stairs
devised by Michelangelo, stairs that are built after
the pattern of downward-gliding waters—broadly
bringing forth step out of step in their descent like
wave out of wave. Through such impressions one
collects oneself, wins oneself back again out of the
pretentious multiplicity that talks and chatters there
(and how talkative it is!), and one learns slowly to
recognize the very few things in which the eternal
endures that one can love and something solitary in
which one can quietly take part.

I am still living in the city, on the Capitol, not
far from the finest equestrian statue that has come
down to us from Roman art—that of Marcus Aurelius; but in a few weeks I shall move into a quiet
simple room, an old flat-roofed summerhouse, that
lies lost way deep in a large park, hidden from the
town, its noise and incident. There I shall live all
winter and rejoice in the great quiet, from which I
expect the gift of good and industrious hours. . . .

From thence, where I shall be more at home,
I will write you a longer letter, further discussing
what you have written me. Today I must only tell
you (and perhaps it is wrong of me not to have done
this before) that the book announced in your letter (which was to contain works of yours) has not
arrived here. Has it gone back to you, perhaps from

Worpswede? (For one may not forward parcels to foreign countries.) This is the most favorable possibility, and I would like to know it confirmed. I hope there is no question of loss—which, the Italian mails being what they are, would not be anything exceptional—unfortunately.

I would have been glad to get this book (as I would anything that gives a sign of you); and verses that you have written meantime I shall always (if you will confide them to me) read and read again and experience as well and as sincerely as I can. With wishes and greetings,

Yours:

RAINER MARIA RILKE

SIX

Rome, December 23rd, 1903

My dear Mr. Kappus,

You shall not be without a greeting from me when Christmas comes and when you, in the midst of the holiday, are bearing your solitude more heavily than usual. But if then you notice that it is great, rejoice because of this; for what (ask yourself) would solitude be that had no greatness; there is but one solitude, and that is great, and not easy to bear, and to almost everybody come hours when they would gladly exchange it for any sort of intercourse, however banal and cheap, for the semblance of some slight accord with the first comer, with the unworthiest. But perhaps those are the very hours when solitude grows;

for its growing is painful as the growing of boys and sad as the beginning of springtimes. But that must not mislead you. The necessary thing is after all but this: solitude, great inner solitude. Going-into-oneself and for hours meeting no one—this one must be able to attain. To be solitary, the way one was solitary as a child, when the grownups went around involved with things that seemed important and big because they themselves looked so busy and because one comprehended nothing of their doings.

And when one day one perceives that their occupations are paltry, their professions petrified and no longer linked with living, why not then continue to look like a child upon it all as upon something unfamiliar, from out of the depth of one's own world, out of the expanse of one's own solitude, which is itself work and status and vocation? Why want to exchange a child's wise incomprehension for defensiveness and disdain, since incomprehension is after all being alone, while defensiveness and disdain are a sharing in that from which one wants by these means to keep apart.

Think, dear sir, of the world you carry within you, and call this thinking what you will; whether it be remembering your own childhood or yearning toward your own future—only be attentive to that which rises up in you and set it above everything that you observe about you. What goes on in your innermost being is worthy of your whole love; you must somehow keep working at it and not lose too much time and too much courage in clarifying your attitude toward people. Who tells you that you have one anyway?— I know, your profession is hard and full of contradiction of yourself, and I foresaw your complaint and knew that it would come. Now that it has come, I cannot comfort you, I can only advise you to consider whether all professions are not like that, full of demands, full of enmity against the individual, saturated as it were with the hatred of those who have found themselves mute and sullen in a humdrum duty. The situation in which you now have to live is no more heavily laden with conventions, prejudices and mistakes than all the other situations, and if there are some that feign a greater freedom, still there is none that is in itself broad and spacious and in contact with the big things of which real living consists. Only the individual who is solitary is like a thing placed under profound laws, and when he goes out into the morning that is just beginning, or looks out into the evening that is full of happening, and if he feels what is going on there, then all status drops from him as from a dead man, though he stands in the midst of sheer life. What you, dear Mr. Kappus, must now experience as an officer, you would have felt just the same in any of the established professions; yes, even if, outside of any position, you had merely sought some light and independent contact with society, this feeling of constraint would not have been spared you.— It is so everywhere; but that is no reason for fear or sorrow; if there is nothing in common between you and other people, try being close to things, they will not desert you; there are the nights still and the winds that go through the trees and across many lands; among things and with the animals everything is still full of happening, in which you may participate; and children are still the way you were as a child, sad like that and happy,—and if you think of your childhood you live among them again, among the solitary children, and the grownups are nothing, and their dignity has no value.

And if it worries and torments you to think of your childhood and of the simplicity and quiet that goes with it, because you cannot believe any more in God, who appears everywhere in it, then ask yourself, dear Mr. Kappus, whether you really have lost God? Is it not rather, that you have never yet possessed him? For when should that have been? Do you believe that a child can hold him, him whom men bear only with effort and whose weight compresses the old? Do you believe that anyone who really has him could lose him like a little stone, or do you not think rather that whoever had him could only be lost by him?— But if you know he was not in your childhood, and not before, if you suspect that Christ was deluded by his longing and Mohammed betrayed by his pride—and if you are terrified to feel that even now he is not, in this hour when we speak of him—what then justifies you in missing him, who never was, like one who has passed away, and in seeking him as though he had been lost?

Why do you not think of him as the coming one, imminent from all eternity, the future one, the final fruit of a tree whose leaves we are? What keeps you from projecting his birth into times that are in process of becoming, and living your life like a painful and beautiful day in the history of a great gestation? For do you not see how everything that happens keeps on being a beginning, and could it not be His beginning, since beginning is in itself always so beautiful? If he is the most perfect, must not the lesser be before him, so that he can choose himself out of fullness and overflow?— Must he not be the last, in order to encompass everything within himself, and what meaning would we have if he, whom we long for, had already been?

As the bees bring in the honey, so do we fetch the sweetest out of everything and build Him. With the trivial even, with the insignificant (if it but happens out of love) we make a start, with work and with rest after it, with a silence or with a small solitary joy, with everything that we do alone, without supporters and participants, we begin him whom we shall not live to know, even as our forebears could not live to know us. And yet they, who are long gone, are in us, as predisposition, as burden upon our destiny, as blood that pulsates, and as gesture that rises up out of the depths of time.

Is there anything that can take from you the hope of thus some day being in him, the farthest, the ultimate?

Celebrate Christmas, dear Mr. Kappus, in this devout feeling, that perhaps He needs this very fear of life from you in order to begin; these very days of your transition are perhaps the time when everything in you is working at him, as you have already once, in childhood, breathlessly worked at him. Be patient and without resentment and think that the least we can do is to make his becoming not more difficult for him than the earth makes it for the spring when it wants to come.

And be glad and confident.

Yours:

RAINER MARIA RILKE

SEVEN

Rome, May 14th, 1904

My dear Mr. Kappus,

Much time has gone by since I received your last letter. Do not hold that against me; first it was work, then interruptions and finally a poor state of health that again and again kept me from the answer, which (so I wanted it) was to come to you out of quiet and good days. Now I feel somewhat better again (the opening of spring with its mean, fitful changes was very trying here too) and come to greet you, dear Mr. Kappus, and to tell you (which I do with all my heart) one thing and another in reply to your letter, as well as I know how.

You see—I have copied your sonnet, because I

found that it is lovely and simple and born in the form in which it moves with such quiet decorum. It is the best of those of your poems that you have let me read. And now I give you this copy because I know that it is important and full of new experience to come upon a work of one's own again written in a strange hand. Read the lines as though they were someone else's, and you will feel deep within you how much they are your own.

It was a pleasure to me to read this sonnet and your letter often; I thank you for both.

And you should not let yourself be confused in your solitude by the fact that there is something in you that wants to break out of it. This very wish will help you, if you use it quietly, and deliberately and like a tool, to spread out your solitude over wide country. People have (with the help of conventions) oriented all their solutions toward the easy and toward the easiest side of the easy; but it is clear that we must hold to what is difficult; everything alive holds to it, everything in Nature grows and defends itself in its own way and is characteristically and spontaneously itself, seeks at all costs to be so and against all opposition. We know little, but that we must hold to what is difficult is a certainty that will not forsake us; it is good to be solitary, for solitude is difficult; that something is difficult must be a reason the more for us to do it.

To love is good, too: love being difficult. For one human being to love another: that is perhaps the most difficult of all our tasks, the ultimate, the last test and proof, the work for which all other work is but preparation. For this reason young people, who are beginners in everything, cannot yet know love: they have to learn it. With their whole being, with all their forces, gathered close about their lonely, timid, upward-beating heart, they must learn to love. But learning-time is always a long, secluded time, and so loving, for a long while ahead and far on into life, is—solitude, intensified and deepened loneness for him who loves. Love is at first not anything that means merging, giving over, and uniting with another (for what would a union be of something unclarified and unfinished, still subordinate—?), it is a high inducement to the individual to ripen, to become something in himself, to become world, to become world for himself for another's sake, it is a great exacting claim upon him, something that chooses him out and calls him to vast things. Only in this sense, as the task of working at themselves ("to hearken and to hammer day and night"), might young people use the love that is given them. Merging and surrendering and every kind of communion is not for them (who must save and gather for a long, long time still), is the ultimate, is perhaps that for which human lives as yet scarcely suffice.

But young people err so often and so grievously in this: that they (in whose nature it lies to have no patience) fling themselves at each other, when love takes possession of them, scatter themselves, just as they are, in all their untidiness, disorder, confusion. . . . And then what? What is life to do to this heap of half-battered existence which they call their communion and which they would gladly call their happiness, if it were possible, and their future? Thus each loses himself for the sake of the other and loses the other and many others that wanted still to come. And loses the expanses and the possibilities, exchanges the approach and flight of gentle, divining things for an unfruitful perplexity out of which nothing can come any more, nothing save a little disgust, disillusionment and poverty, and rescue in one of the many conventions that have been put up in great number like public refuges along this most dangerous road. No realm of human experience is so well provided with conventions as this: life-preservers of most varied invention, boats and swimming-bladders are here; the social conception has managed to supply shelters of every sort, for, as it was disposed to take love-life as a pleasure, it had also to give it an easy form, cheap, safe and sure, as public pleasures are.

It is true that many young people who love wrongly, that is, simply with abandon and unsolitarily (the average will of course always go on doing so), feel the oppressiveness of a failure and want to make the situation in which they have landed viable and fruitful in their own personal way—; for their nature tells them that, less even than all else that is important, can questions of love be solved publicly and according to this or that agreement; that they are questions, intimate questions from one human being to another, which in any case demand a new, special, only personal answer—: but how should they, who have already flung themselves together and no longer mark off and distinguish themselves from each other, who therefore no longer possess anything of their own selves, be able to find a way out of themselves, out of the depth of their already shattered solitude?

They act out of common helplessness, and then, if, with the best intentions, they try to avoid the convention that occurs to them (say, marriage), they land in the tentacles of some less loud, but equally deadly conventional solution; for then everything far around them is—convention; where people act out of a prematurely fused, turbid communion, every move is convention: every relation to which such entanglement leads has its convention, be it ever so unusual (that is, in the ordinary sense immoral); why, even separation would here be a conventional step, an impersonal chance decision without strength and without fruit.

Whoever looks seriously at it finds that neither for death, which is difficult, nor for difficult love has any explanation, any solution, any hint or way yet been discerned; and for these two problems that we carry wrapped up and hand on without opening, it will not be possible to discover any general rule resting in agreement. But in the same measure in which we begin as individuals to put life to the test, we shall, being individuals, meet these great things at closer range. The demands which the difficult work of love makes upon our development are more than life-size, and as beginners we are not up to them. But if we nevertheless hold out and take this love upon us as burden and apprenticeship, instead of losing ourselves in all the light and frivolous play, behind which people have hidden from the most earnest earnestness of their existence—then a little progress and an alleviation will perhaps be perceptible to those who come long after us; that would be much.

We are only just now beginning to look upon the relation of one individual person to a second individual objectively and without prejudice, and our attempts to live such associations have no model before them. And yet in the changes brought about by time there is already a good deal that would help our timorous novitiate.

The girl and the woman, in their new, their own unfolding, will but in passing be imitators of masculine ways, good and bad, and repeaters of masculine professions. After the uncertainty of such transitions it will become apparent that women were only going through the profusion and the vicissitude of those (often ridiculous) disguises in order to cleanse their own most characteristic nature of the distorting influences of the other sex. Women, in whom life lingers and dwells more immediately, more fruitfully and more confidently, must surely have become fundamentally riper people, more human people, than easygoing man, who is not pulled down below the surface of life by the weight of any fruit of his body, and who, presumptuous and hasty, undervalues what he thinks he loves. This humanity of woman, borne its full time in suffering and humiliation, will come to light when she will have stripped off the conventions of mere femininity in the mutations of her outward status, and those men who do not yet feel it approaching today will be surprised and struck by it. Some day (and for this, particularly in the northern countries, reliable signs are already speaking and shining), some day there will be girls and women whose name will no longer signify merely an opposite of the masculine, but something in itself, something that makes one think, not of any complement and limit, but only of life and existence: the feminine human being.

This advance will (at first much against the will of the outstripped men) change the love-experience, which is now full of error, will alter it from the ground up, reshape it into a relation that is meant to be of one human being to another, no longer of man to woman. And this more human love (that will fulfill itself, infinitely considerate and gentle, and kind and clear in binding and releasing) will resemble that which we are preparing with struggle and toil, the love that consists in this, that two solitudes protect and border and salute each other.

And this further: do not believe that that great love once enjoined upon you, the boy, was lost; can you say whether great and good desires did not ripen in you at the time, and resolutions by which you are still living today? I believe that that love remains so strong and powerful in your memory because it was your first deep being-alone and the first inward work you did on your life.— All good wishes for you, dear Mr. Kappus!

Yours:
RAINER MARIA RILKE

SONETT

Durch mein Leben zittert ohne Klage,
ohne Seufzer ein tiefdunkles Weh.
Meiner Träume reiner Blüthenschnee
ist die Weihe meiner stillsten Tage.

Öfter aber kreuzt die grosse Frage
meinen Pfad. Ich werde klein und geh
kalt vorüber wie an einem See,
dessen Flut ich nicht zu messen wage.

Und dann sinkt ein Leid auf mich, so trübe
wie das Grau glanzarmer Sommernächte,
die ein Stern durchflimmert—dann und wann—:

Meine Hände tasten dann nach Liebe,
weil ich gerne Laute beten möchte,
die mein heisser Mund nicht finden kann. . . .

(FRANZ KAPPUS)

SONNET

Through my life there trembles without plaint,
without a sigh a deep-dark melancholy.
The pure and snowy blossoming of my dreams
is the consecration of my stillest days.

But oftentimes the great question crosses
my path. I become small and go
coldly past as though along some lake
whose flood I have not hardihood to measure.

And then a sorrow sinks upon me, dusky
as the gray of lusterless summer nights
through which a star glimmers—now and then—:

My hands then gropingly reach out for love,
because I want so much to pray sounds
that my hot mouth cannot find. . . .

EIGHT

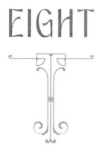

Borgeby gård, Flãdie, Sweden,
August 12th, 1904

I want to talk to you again a while, dear Mr. Kappus, although I can say almost nothing that is helpful, hardly anything useful. You have had many and great sadnesses, which passed. And you say that even this passing was hard for you and put you out of sorts. But, please, consider whether these great sadnesses have not rather gone right through the center of yourself? Whether much in you has not altered, whether you have not somewhere, at some point of your being, undergone a change while you were sad? Only those sadnesses are dangerous and bad which one carries about among people in order to drown them out; like sicknesses that are superficially and foolishly treated they simply withdraw and after a little pause break out again the more dreadfully; and accumulate within one and are life, are unlived, spurned, lost life, of which one may die. Were it possible for us to see further than our knowledge reaches, and yet a little way beyond the outworks of our divining, perhaps we would endure our sadnesses with greater confidence than our joys. For they are the moments when something new has entered into us, something unknown; our feelings grow mute in shy perplexity, everything in us withdraws, a stillness comes, and the new, which no one knows, stands in the midst of it and is silent.

I believe that almost all our sadnesses are moments of tension that we find paralyzing because we no longer hear our surprised feelings living. Because we are alone with the alien thing that has entered into our self; because everything intimate and accustomed is for an instant taken away; because we stand in the middle of a transition where we cannot remain standing. For this reason the sadness too passes: the new thing in us, the added thing, has entered into our heart, has gone into its inmost chamber and is not even there any more,—is already in our blood. And we do not learn what it was. We could easily be made to believe that nothing has happened, and yet we have changed, as a house changes into which a guest has entered. We cannot say who has come, perhaps we shall never know, but many signs indicate that the future enters into us in this way in order to transform itself in us long before it happens. And this is why it is so important to be lonely and attentive when one is sad: because the apparently uneventful and stark moment at which our future sets foot in us is so much closer to life than that other noisy and fortuitous point of time at which it happens to us as if from outside. The more still, more patient and more open we are when we are sad, so much the deeper and so much the more unswervingly does the new go into us, so much the better do we make it ours, so much the more will it be our destiny, and when on some later day it "happens" (that is, steps forth out of us to others), we shall feel in our inmost selves akin and near to it. And that is necessary. It is necessary—and toward this our development will move gradually— that nothing strange should befall us, but only that which has long belonged to us. We have already had to rethink so many of our concepts of motion, we will also gradually learn to realize that that which we call destiny goes forth from within people, not from without into them. Only because so many have not absorbed their destinies and transmuted them within themselves while they were living in them, have they not recognized what has gone forth out of them; it was so strange to them that, in their bewildered fright, they thought it must only just then have entered into them, for they swear never before to have found anything like it in themselves. As people were long mistaken about the motion of the sun, so they are even yet mistaken about the motion of that which is to come. The future stands firm, dear Mr. Kappus, but we move in infinite space.

How should it not be difficult for us?

And to speak of solitude again, it becomes always clearer that this is at bottom not something that one can take or leave. We are solitary. We may delude ourselves and act as though this were not so. That is all. But how much better it is to realize that we are so, yes, even to begin by assuming it. We shall indeed turn dizzy then; for all points upon which our eye has been accustomed to rest are taken from us, there is nothing near any more and everything far is infinitely far. A person removed from his own room, almost without preparation and transition, and set upon the height of a great mountain range, would feel something of the sort: an unparalleled insecurity, an abandonment to something inexpressible would almost annihilate him. He would think himself falling or hurled out into space, or exploded into a thousand pieces: what a monstrous lie his brain would have to invent to catch up with and explain the state of his senses! So for him who becomes solitary all distances, all measures change; of these changes many take place suddenly, and then, as with the man on the mountaintop, extraordinary imaginings and singular sensations arise that seem to grow out beyond all bearing. But it is necessary for us to experience that too. We must assume our existence as broadly as we in any way can; everything, even the unheard-of, must be possible in it. That is at bottom the only courage that is demanded of us: to have courage for the most strange, the most singular and the most inexplicable that we may encounter. That mankind has in this sense been cowardly has done life endless harm; the experiences that are called "visions," the whole so-called "spirit-world," death, all those things that are so closely akin to us, have by daily parrying been so crowded out of life that the senses with which we could have grasped them are atrophied. To say nothing of God. But fear of the inexplicable has not alone impoverished the existence of the individual; the relationship between one human being and another has also been cramped by it, as though it had been lifted out of the riverbed of endless possibilities and set down in a fallow spot on the bank, to which nothing happens. For it is not inertia alone that is responsible for human relationships repeating themselves from case to case, indescribably monotonous and unrenewed; it is shyness before any sort of new, unforeseeable experience with which one does not think oneself able to cope. But only someone who is ready for everything, who excludes nothing, not even the most enigmatical, will live the relation to another as something alive and will himself draw exhaustively from his own existence. For if we think of this existence of the individual as a larger or smaller room, it appears evident that most people learn to know only a corner of their room, a place by the window, a strip of floor on which they walk up and down. Thus they have a certain security. And yet that dangerous insecurity is so much more human which drives the prisoners in Poe's stories to feel out the shapes of their horrible dungeons and not be strangers to the unspeakable terror of their abode. We, however, are not prisoners. No traps or snares are set about us, and there is nothing which should intimidate or worry us. We are set down in life as in the element to which we best correspond, and over and above this we have through thousands of years of accommodation become so like this life, that when we hold still we are, through a happy mimicry, scarcely to be distinguished from all that surrounds us. We have no reason to mistrust our world, for it is not against us. Has it terrors, they are our terrors; has it abysses, those abysses belong to us; are dangers at hand, we must try to love them. And if only we arrange our life according to that principle which counsels us that we must always hold to the difficult, then that which now still seems to us the most alien will become what we most trust and find most faithful. How should we be able to forget those ancient myths that are at the beginning of all peoples, the myths about dragons that at the last moment turn into princesses; perhaps all the dragons of our lives are princesses who are only waiting to see us once beautiful and brave. Perhaps everything terrible is in its deepest being something helpless that wants help from us.

So you must not be frightened, dear Mr. Kappus, if a sadness rises up before you larger than any you have ever seen; if a restiveness, like light and cloud-shadows, passes over your hands and over all you do. You must think that something is happening with you, that life has not forgotten you, that it holds you in its hand; it will not let you fall. Why do you want to shut out of your life any agitation, any pain, any melancholy, since you really do not know what these states are working upon you? Why do you want to persecute yourself with the question whence all this may be coming and whither it is bound? Since you know that you are in the midst of transitions and wished for nothing so much as to change. If there is anything morbid in your processes, just remember that sickness is the means by which an organism frees itself of foreign matter; so one must just help it to be sick, to have its whole sickness and break out with it, for that is its progress. In you, dear Mr. Kappus, so much is now happening; you must be patient as a sick man and confident as a convalescent; for perhaps you are both. And more: you are the doctor too, who has to watch over himself. But there are in every illness many days when the doctor can do nothing but wait. And this it is that you, insofar as you are your own doctor, must now above all do.

Do not observe yourself too much. Do not draw too hasty conclusions from what happens to you; let it simply happen to you. Otherwise you will too easily look with reproach (that is, morally) upon your past, which naturally has its share in all that you are now meeting. But that part of the errors, desires and longings of your boyhood which is working in you is not what you remember and condemn. The unusual conditions of a lonely and helpless childhood are so difficult, so complicated, open to so many influences and at the same time so disengaged from all real connections with life that, where a vice enters into it, one may not without more ado simply call it vice. One must be so careful with names anyway; it is so often on the name of a misdeed that a life goes to pieces, not the nameless and personal action itself, which was perhaps a perfectly definite necessity of that life and would have been absorbed by it without effort. And the expenditure of energy seems to you so great only because you overvalue victory; it is not the victory that is the "great thing" you think to have done, although you are right in your feeling; the great thing is that there was already something there which you could put in the place of that delusion, something true and real. Without this even your victory would have been but a moral reaction, without wide significance, but thus it has become a segment of your life. Your life, dear Mr. Kappus, of which I think with so many wishes. Do you remember how that life yearned out of its childhood for the "great"? I see that it is now going on beyond the great to long for greater. For this reason it will not cease to be difficult, but for this reason too it will not cease to grow.

And if there is one thing more that I must say to you, it is this: do not believe that he who seeks to comfort you lives untroubled among the simple and quiet words that sometimes do you good. His life has much difficulty and sadness and remains far behind yours. Were it otherwise he would never have been able to find those words.

Yours:

RAINER MARIA RILKE

NINE

Furuborg, Jonsered, in Sweden,
November 4th, 1904

My dear Mr. Kappus,

In this time that has gone by without a letter I have
been partly traveling, partly so busy that I could not
write. And even today writing comes hard to me
because I have already had to write a lot of letters so
that my hand is tired. If I could dictate, I would say
a great deal to you, but as it is, take only a few words
for your long letter.

I think of you, dear Mr. Kappus, often and with
such concentrated wishes that that really ought to
help you somehow. Whether my letters can really be
a help, I often doubt. Do not say: yes, they are. Just

accept them and without much thanks, and let us await what comes.

There is perhaps no use my going into your particular points now; for what I could say about your tendency to doubt or about your inability to bring outer and inner life into unison, or about all the other things that worry you—: it is always what I have already said: always the wish that you may find patience enough in yourself to endure, and simplicity enough to believe; that you may acquire more and more confidence in that which is difficult, and in your solitude among others. And for the rest, let life happen to you. Believe me: life is right, in any case.

And about emotions: all emotions are pure which gather you and lift you up; that emotion is impure which seizes only one side of your being and so distorts you. Everything that you can think in the face of your childhood, is right. Everything that makes more of you than you have heretofore been in your best hours, is right. Every heightening is good if it is in your whole blood, if it is not intoxication, not turbidity, but joy which one can see clear to the bottom. Do you understand what I mean?

And your doubt may become a good quality if you train it. It must become knowing, it must become critical. Ask it, whenever it wants to spoil something for you, why something is ugly, demand proofs from it, test it, and you will find it perplexed and embarrassed perhaps, or perhaps rebellious. But don't give in, insist on arguments and act this way, watchful and consistent, every single time, and the day will arrive when from a destroyer it will become one of your best workers—perhaps the cleverest of all that are building at your life.

That is all, dear Mr. Kappus, that I am able to tell you today. But I am sending you at the same time the reprint of a little poetical work* that has now appeared in the Prague periodical *Deutsche Arbeit.* There I speak to you further of life and of death and of how both are great and splendid.

Yours:

RAINER MARIA RILKE

---

* *The Lay of the Love and Death of Cornet Otto* [subsequent editions: *Christoph*] *Rilke,* familiarly and very widely known as "the *Cornet,*" had been written in 1899.

TEN

Paris, the day after Christmas, 1908

You must know, dear Mr. Kappus, how glad I was to have that lovely letter from you. The news you give me, real and tellable as it now is again, seems good to me, and, the longer I have thought it over, the more I have felt it to be in fact good. I really wanted to write you this for Christmas Eve; but what with work, in which I am living this winter, variously and uninterruptedly, the ancient holiday approached so fast that I had hardly any time left to attend to the most necessary errands, much less to write.

But I have thought of you often during these holidays and imagined how quiet you must be in your lonely fort among the empty hills, upon which those big southerly winds precipitate themselves as though they would devour them in great pieces.

The stillness must be immense in which such sounds and movements have room, and when one thinks that to it all the presence of the far-off sea comes chiming in as well, perhaps as the inmost tone in that prehistoric harmony, then one can only wish for you that you are confidently and patiently letting that lofty solitude work upon you which is no more to be stricken out of your life; which in every-thing there is ahead of you to experience and to do will work as an anonymous influence, continuously and gently decisive, much as in us blood of ancestors ceaselessly stirs and mingles with our own into that unique, not repeatable being which at every turning of our life we are.

Yes: I am glad you have that steady expressible existence with you, that title, that uniform, that ser-vice, all that tangible and limited reality, which in such surroundings, with a similarly isolated and not numerous command, takes on seriousness and neces-sity, implies a vigilant application above and beyond the military profession's tendency to play and to pass the time, and not only allows but actually cultivates a self-reliant attentiveness. And to be among condi-tions that work at us, that set us before big natural things from time to time, is all we need.

Art too is only a way of living, and, however one lives, one can, unwittingly, prepare oneself for it; in all that is real one is closer to it and more nearly neighbored than in the unreal half-artistic professions, which, while they pretend proximity to some art, in practice belie and assail the existence of all art, as for instance the whole of journalism does and almost all criticism and three-quarters of what is called and wants to be called literature. I am glad, in a word, that you have surmounted the danger of falling into this sort of thing and are somewhere in a rough reality being solitary and courageous. May the year that is at hand uphold and strengthen you in that.

Ever yours:

RAINER MARIA RILKE

CHRONICLE,
1903-1908

*The life of one that laboureth and is
contented shall be made sweet.*

—Ecclesiasticus

INTRODUCTION

When the Young Poet made his appeal to Rilke, he must
have had some inkling of the sort of sympathy he might
look for, but he could scarcely have realized what dis-
cords of bitter memory he had jarred. Perhaps no single
episode of his youth had left such lasting impress upon
Rilke's development as his experience at military school;
hence its importance in relation to that later period in
which the *Letters to a Young Poet* fall. He had been sent to
Sankt-Pölten as a matter of course by a conventional officer father and a self-absorbed, religious-fanatical mother
who in her letters only excited him to further unhappi-
ness with expressions of sympathy and seemed to have no
idea of mending the situation either by strengthening him
to endure the ordeal or by removing him. Although he

entered in good condition, sunburned and well after summer holidays and of normal development for his age, he was by temperament totally unfitted to stand the physical discipline of any such establishment and, which was even worse, soon became the victim of his comrades' active and often cruel contempt. Doubtless they found him a romantic sentimentalist and prig, for which his early childhood would have been much to blame. Any ten- or twelve- or fourteen-year-old boy who, on being vigorously struck in the face, could say "in a quiet voice . . . 'I endure it because Christ endured it, silently and without complaint, and while you were hitting me I prayed my good God to forgive you,'" need have expected nothing but the derisive laughter of his contemporaries. But this sort of thing drove him to nights of weeping, to far too many days in the infirmary, "more spiritually afflicted," he says himself, "than physically ill." It drove him also to writing poetry "which already in its childish beginnings comforted" him—very fiery and noble and not at all original poetry, but still his most natural form of response to his environment and refuge from it.

Many years later, in the fall of 1920, Rilke received a letter from a Major-General Sedlakowitz, who had taught him German at the Sankt-Pölten school and who, having recently heard Ellen Key lecture on the prominent lyric poet, ventured to express his admiration and to recall his early sympathy (even though he had applied considerable

red ink to the imaginative essays of his pupil). He hoped
for an answer—even a short answer. Rilke's reply covers,
against his two pages, eight.* It is uncompromising and
courageous and truthful, charming and kind; such a letter as only one who cared for honesty and had a fine sense
of delicacy in human relationships would have troubled to
write. He is grateful for his correspondent's desire to renew
acquaintance, but tells him straight from the shoulder that
he feels he would never have been able to make what he
has of his life had he not totally suppressed for decades
all recollection of those five years at military school; there
were times when the least memory of them threatened
the new creative consciousness for which he strove, and
he has never been able to understand this visitation of his
childhood. If his attitude seems exaggerated he begs the
Major-General to remember that he had left the school
exhausted, physically and spiritually misused and retarded
at sixteen, deprived of strength for the great task ahead of
him, totally misprepared, and growing always more aware
of how different an introduction to life he should have had,
suffering from the sense that the time and effort spent in
those preparatory years were irretrievable. He would like
to acknowledge any friendly incident that chanced to

---

* Both letters are given in full in Carl Sieber's *René Rilke* (Insel Verlag,
Leipzig, 1932). Rilke's reply is included in both editions of the *Briefe* (Insel
Verlag, Leipzig), and in volume II of the *Letters*, translated by J. B. Greene
and M. D. Herter Norton (W. W. Norton & Company, Inc., New York, 1948).

befall him during that time, but anything of the sort was so scarce that it seems only natural he should have sought protection in later moments of his youth by including the whole experience "in the feeling of one single terrible damnation."

Rilke never put through the military novel he had it in mind to write and the only descriptions he left, outside of his letters, are fragments.[*] But this mature statement is evidence enough that the experiences of Sankt-Pölten and Mährisch-Weisskirchen amounted to more than child-ish discomfort, to much more than mere uncongeniality. One might ask, who knows to what extent they caused the crystallizing out of his individual characteristics? For it is to be noted that he showed a typical loyalty to duty and self-discipline, and no inconsiderable strength of will, in enduring them. Furthermore, they did not embitter him, much as he shrank and was appalled; they seem only to have opened up—as counterbalance perhaps to his ulti-mate sensitivity and exaltation of thought—his peculiar awareness of human misery, that most acute misery of mind and spirit which despair and fear of whatever sort, psychological if not bodily, may engender.

---

[*] See "Die Turnstunde," chief of these, in *Gesammelte Werke*, IV (Insel Verlag, 1927), and, together with an earlier version, in *Sämmtliche Werke*, IV (1961). Carl Sieber's *René Rilke* (Insel Verlag, 1932) gives it (also "Pierre Dumont" and "Erin-nerung") as written in the Schmargendorf Diary, Nov. 5, 1899. Carl Niemeyer's *R. M. Rilke: Primal Sound and Other Prose Pieces* (Cummington Press, Cum-mington, Mass., 1943) contains an English translation, "Gym Period."

INTERIM

He left, with his father's approval, in the spring of 1891 (at fifteen and a half) to found himself "a new career" in a more congenial manner. It is not surprising that a youth with the makings of a poet, and especially a Rilke, should have been a misfit in such a place. But it is surprising that Rilke himself should have taken it for granted he was to become an officer even during the first part of the ensuing study years, while external influences, it is to be assumed, were stronger with him than his awareness of himself; or perhaps it would be truer to say, before his conviction of his own singularity—for it did uphold him even during the school time, this *knowing* that he was not of or for the life of others—had stamped itself undeniably upon his external world. While staying now with his Uncle Jaroslav in the suburb of Smichov, lying in the garden and wandering *en flâneur* about Prague, he still wore his uniform on his walks "because in these villages one is more respected." In the next winter at Linz, where he went to attend the business academy, he composed his first poem to be printed, a swinging, martial glorification of war in answer to the Baroness von Suttner's "Lay Down Your Arms!" No human individuality ever underwent greater change than Rilke's did in the next ten years. This partly explains why at twenty-eight, with all his artist's wisdom, he was still searching for his own foothold; how throughout his life, while so determined, he was still so unestablished.

Back in Prague, he studied, privately at first and later at the Carl-Ferdinand University: religion, philosophy, German, history of art and of literature, and even the beginnings of the law. He also read enormously: Goethe, Rückert, Lenau, Shakespeare, Schopenhauer, Tolstoi. He seems to have been busy and happy on the whole. His first love affairs fall in this period: an amorous escapade with a governess in Linz which he soon saw as an "alberne Liebe-lei" (silly flirtation) of which he was well rid; and the three years' association of stimulating companionship, work, inspiration, and romance with Valery David-Rhonfeld, significant for him, whatever it may have meant to her, since under her influence (daughter of an Austrian artil-lery officer living in the Weinberge section of Prague, she "painted vases and wrote stories and combined the two with the eccentric behavior of genius," says Sieber) he reacted definitely and forever away from the conventional class-consciousness of the army in his desire to become an artist. All the time he was writing. First, at the second vol-ume of a history (not extant) of the Thirty Years' War, the significance of which he apparently saw as the revealing of great men, heroes, against the background of events. Then always poems, very reminiscent, only here and there char-acteristic of himself because he could not bear to publish the things he really cared for and put forth only the least personal. One volume, *Leben und Lieder* (*Life and Songs*), was published in 1894 with money Valery put up; and two issues of *Wegwarten* (*Chicory*, which "Paracelsus says turns every hundred years into a living being," so Rilke hopes his poems "may wake to higher life in the soul of the people"), he published himself and with a sentimental-idealistic gesture gave away to hospitals and free libraries; and he also published* in various periodicals, on one of which he acted for a time as editor. Finally, and with great seriousness, dramatic sketches of a theatric-emotional kind, which totally failed. The only product of these years which Rilke thought worthy of inclusion in the *Gesammelte Werke* is *Larenopfer* (*Offerings to the Lares*), originally published at Christmas 1896 while he was studying in Munich, a collection of poems for the most part only conventional German-lyric in form and content but colored by feeling for his native Bohemia and here and there already more personal. *Traumgekrönt* (*Dream-Crowned*) he published in 1897, and *Advent* in 1898.

After some brief but contented study at the University of Berlin, Rilke set out in the spring of 1899 for Moscow with his friend Lou Andreas-Salomé. Twice he went to Russia, the second time just a year later. These two trips, during which he not only traveled and drank deep of the

---

* The short stories are to be found in *Erzählungen und Skizzen aus der Frühzeit* (Insel Verlag, 1928) and, with a few not before published, in *Sämmtliche Werke*, IV (1961).

scene and atmosphere of the country, but met Tolstoi, and Droschin the peasant poet, and many other people in the intellectual and artistic world, left an impression upon him (he was twenty-three and twenty-four) which so penetrated his creative imagination that its influence is to be sensed in his concepts throughout and to the last. "Russia was reality and at once the deep, daily perceiving that reality is something distant that comes infinitely slowly to those who have patience. Russia, the land where the people are solitary people, each with a world in himself, each full of darkness like a mountain, each deep in his humility, without fear of abasing himself, and therefore reverent. People full of distance, uncertainty and hope: evolving people. And over all a never defined, ever changing, growing God." Some of the *Stories of God** give evidence of what he felt.

On his return from the second trip (1900) Rilke visited Heinrich Vogeler, the painter, in Worpswede, an artists' colony near Bremen. Here he wrote many of the poems that were to appear in *Das Buch der Bilder* (*The Book of Pictures*), the first edition of which came out in the spring of 1902. The associations of this time have been credited with much influence upon Rilke's point of view, and not without justification. But in any such consideration it should be

---

* *Geschichten vom lieben Gott*, first published at Christmas, 1900, under the title *Vom lieben Gott und Anderes (An Grosse für Kinder erzählt)*.

borne in mind that "the essential nature of 'influence' in his case implies an expansion of what is already present in his genius, not the imposition from without of the artistic creed of others, a fact which is of supreme importance in all Rilke criticism, and one which tends to be obscured by his characteristic fashion of giving himself up entirely, for the time being, to each great new experience in his artistic life."[*]

While at Worpswede he met the young sculptress Clara Westhoff, of a Bremen family, to whom he was married in the following year, making his home with her in nearby Westerwede, where in December their daughter Ruth was born. Here he wrote his book on the group of Worpswede painters, published in 1902. During this period it was, and undoubtedly owing in part to his interest in his wife's work, that he came upon the idea which led him to undertake for Richard Muther's series of monographs a study of Rodin.

LETTER ONE

He went to Paris toward the end of August 1902 with the purpose of preparing himself for this agreeable task, and

---

[*] G. Craig Houston, "Rilke's *Buch der Bilder,*" *Modern Language Review,* XXIX, 3, July 1934.

incidentally of studying at the libraries under the guidance of the Vicomte de Vogüé, the French historian and critic, who was a connoisseur of things Russian. Rilke at this time spoke French only haltingly, although he had been brushing up at the Berlitz School in Bremen before coming, and this caused him to be shy at first of meeting people and gave him particular embarrassment when he first met Rodin. He says that the omnipotence of the language saddened him, but it must have been a challenge, for he was already writing verse in French.

We know from the poignant observation in his descriptions that he was busy taking in all the external details that make the charm of that irresistible city—bridges, streets, soft skies, smells, sounds and sights, buildings, populace— and that in later years and in other moods he felt drawn to Paris. But his first impressions were little short of terrible. He found the city strange, inimical, resembling in its excitements, its iniquities and beauties, those biblical cities which the Lord rose up to destroy. He felt alone and rejected of these people, frightened in the foreign turmoil and all the implications of their lives, yet through his sympathy and interest in humanity's concerns torn out of himself into their existences. The newspapers shocked him with their exciting accounts of crime, show-windows with pictorial expositions of disease; he understood why "hospitals are always occurring in Verlaine and Baudelaire and Mallarmé." Much of this feeling about Paris is of course

recorded in the *Aufzeichnungen des Malte Laurids Brigge*,[*]
and many of the episodes there noted are, notwithstand-
ing Rilke's wish that the book as a whole should not be so
regarded, directly autobiographical. Before going to sleep,
for example, he would read the 30th chapter of Job, which
he says entirely expressed his own state, and in the night
he would seek consolation in Baudelaire's *Petits poèmes en
prose*, especially that one which runs "Enfin! la tyrannie de
la face humaine a disparu, et je ne souffrirai plus que par
moi-même," and closes with the paragraph "Mécontent de
tous . . ." quoted in the *Notebooks*. Paris, he wrote only a few
months later, "was for me a similar experience to the military school; as in those days a great fearful astonishment
seized me, so now the terror seized me again before all that
which, as in an indescribable confusion, is called life."

He lived at first at number 11 rue Toullier—a brief little
street close above the Sorbonne—the address which heads
the opening of the *Notebooks*. Undoubtedly some of the
gloom of these early impressions must have been encouraged by his surroundings: a dingy little Latin Quarter
hotel, too much in the midst of the student world, in a
depressingly narrow street which brought many opposite
windows too near to his own, his evenings lighted by a
smelly and wavering kerosene lamp. He moved after a few

---

[*] *The Notebooks of Malte Laurids Brigge* (W. W. Norton & Company, Inc., New
York, 1949), formerly translated as *The Journal of My Other Self*.

weeks to another little hotel nearby, at number 3 rue de l'Abbé de l'Épée, where he was living at the time of the first of these *Letters to a Young Poet*, and whence from his fifth-floor balcony he looked over gardens, then rows of houses, to the dome of the Panthéon, ". . . and sky and morning and evening, space." But even here the atmosphere oppressed him as much as before. In judging of his susceptibility to what are sometimes called morbid impressions, it is to be remembered that Rilke came—not strong and certainly hypersensitive by disposition to noise, to ugliness, to the physical wear of complex surroundings— from the quiet of a German-speaking lowland country to live, practically for the first time, alone to begin with and but a step removed from poverty, in the heart of one of the world's great cities; which fact by itself would account for a good deal of his sense of confusion and shock and dread. For he was not yet anchored in himself and in his work; he was one of those to whom such anchorage was forever being denied.

He had come with a purpose, however, and the difficulties made him only the more determined to stay, because he felt that if he once got into work there, it would be very deeply, and for this he was waiting, preparing. His hours had been full of occupation. He would spend days at the Bibliothèque Nationale, reading French literature and history, or examining reproductions of twelfth- and thirteenth-century cathedrals. Other days he would spend in museums studying pictures and sculpture, acquainting himself in preparation for his work on Rodin with the antique, the classic, the modern, seeing for the first time the great Botticellis and Leonardos, the Venus de Milo (which was "too modern" for him), the Nike of Samothrace (which, on the other hand, expressed the true Greece to him), the graceful world of Tanagra. The Panthéon he found a "kindly place"; Notre-Dame grew upon him every day. It was a most important period in his development.

And to all the disturbance Rodin was a "great, quiet, powerful contradiction." Behind his own restless unease Rilke was experiencing the influence that radiated from the immense calm strength of this great creative personality, that seemed to shelter him under its colossal impress "from the thousandfold fears that came later." Perhaps the most important single element for him in their association at this time, came through Rodin's philosophy of "toujours travailler" which Rilke so touchingly, and ever and again so vainly, sought to exemplify in his own life. For occupation however intent, study, reading, the pursuit of education or of information, have not for the artist that utmost satisfaction which both elates and calms, both inspires and exhausts, and which comes only with his own creative activity. Here was Rodin, in daily and continuous preoccupation hewing and molding the visions of near a lifetime with that lifetime's acquired skill, while the poet Rilke was passing through a period of frustration.

. . . very alone and very forsaken I go my way; and of course that is good: I never wanted it otherwise. But all the fear and worry that came and grew with the happiness and the largess of the past year, has made that in me which creates weak and uncertain and timid. But I am a very defenseless creature (because I was a very timid, lost, defenseless child), and when fate cries out to me I always grow quite, quite still for a long time and must remain so, even though I suffer unspeakably day and night from the no-longer-sounding. Should one perhaps seek rescue in some quiet handicraft and not be fearful for whatever fruit may be ripening deep within one, behind all the rouse and stir? Sometimes I think it would be a way out, because I see always more clearly that for a person like me nothing is harder and more dangerous than trying to earn his living by writing. I cannot force myself like that to write at all; and the consciousness alone that some relation exists between my writing and the nourishment and needs of the day is enough to make work impossible for me. I must wait in stillness for the sounding. I know that if I force it it will not come at all. (It has come so seldom in the last two years.) . . . [O]n bad days I have only dead words, and they are so corpse-heavy that I cannot write with them, not even a letter. Is that bad, weak? And yet God wills it so with me.

Thus he wrote to Ellen Key on February 13th, 1903, four days before the first of these *Letters to a Young Poet*. What notion of this state of mind could the youthful Kappus possibly have had? There may be by nature little in common between an artist who weaves his visions into words and one who transfers his through the sturdy and concrete technicalities of sculpture, yet something like the guiding assurance that Rilke could hold before young Kappus he was himself drawing now from Rodin.

LETTER TWO

As the Parisian winter worked no good to his health, he fled in March to a warmer climate, to the sea at Viareggio, not far from Pisa—the spot near which almost a hundred years earlier, after the sad wrecking of the *Ariel*, Shelley's body was cast upon the pine-trimmed sandy shore. Rilke had been here before, in the spring of 1898, and had at that time written the *Lieder der Mädchen* (*Girls' Songs*) and the first draft of the *Weisse Fürstin* (*The White Princess*). During the present sojourn he was to be seen wandering about with his Bible and his Jacobsen (*Niels Lyhne*), in retreat from the persistent English and German tourist chatter of the Hotel Florence, finding solitary refreshment in sunbaths and ocean plunges and barefoot walks along untenanted stretches of the beach. He describes his costume as a black-and-red-striped bathing-suit of which he wore only the trunks, keeping the top "to pull on in case of emergency, and the emergency is the Englishwoman who may bob up anywhere." The sea did him good; "it cleanses me with its noise and lays a rhythm upon everything in me that is disturbed and confused." When at times, to his surprise, it seemed not so beneficial, "too loud and too incessant," he would withdraw into the woods where he had found a great reclining tree root on which he "sat for hours as alone as on the first day of the world." He very soon wrote to Clara: "I already feel my solitude again a little and suspect that it will deny me nothing if I hearken to it with new strength." And again, a fortnight later: "Everyone must find in his work the center of his life and thence be able to grow out radially as far as may be. And no one else may watch him in the process . . . for not even he himself may do that. There is a kind of cleanness and virginity in it, in this looking away from oneself; it is as though one were drawing, one's gaze bound to the object, inwoven with Nature, while one's hand goes its own way somewhere below, goes on and on, gets timid, wavers, is glad again, goes on and on far below the face that stands like a star above it, not looking, only shining. I feel as though I had always worked that way; face gazing at far things, hands alone. And so it surely ought to be. I shall be like that again in time."

LETTER THREE

This awakening creative urge found its outlet in the writing of parts of the *Stundenbuch* (*Book of Hours*). He delayed his return to Paris because of it, feeling that however slight it might prove to be it would not be good "to go with it in the great railway train and to new impressions in Genoa and Dijon"; while if it came to nothing it would be "better to experience the little disappointment here, knowing that it was not one's own fault." He went back at the end of April, having "done nothing here but write a few letters and read Walter Pater's *Imaginary Portraits* and a bad boring book by the Russian Merejkowski on Leonardo."

LETTER FOUR

The plan to write a monograph on Eugène Carrière which was now in his mind, never came to anything. He did not stay long this time, although he "kept feeling that Paris must present me with another work." Summer drove him thence again, with Clara, to a few peaceful weeks in the flat lands of Worpswede, spent in the white house of their friend Vogeler. He now, on July 18th, two days after writing Letter Four, set down in a long account to Lou Andreas-

Salomé what was, as it were, filling another segment of his consciousness, a detailed description of the effects Paris had had on him, giving us the first sustained intimation of what was to come in *The Notebooks of Malte Laurids Brigge.* Three weeks later— having gone at the end of July to visit "our little Ruth who has her little life not far from here," at Oberneuland, where she lived with Clara's parents—he wrote to this same great friend, to whom he revealed many of his inner dilemmas and much concerning the stages of his growth: ". . . O Lou, in one poem that I succeed with there is more reality than in any relation or inclination that I feel. Where I create I am true, and I want to find the strength to build my life wholly upon this truth, upon this infinite simplicity and joy that is sometimes given me. . . . But how shall I begin . . . ?" He knows—he is now twenty-seven—that he still lacks the discipline for which he longs in order to work. "Have I not the strength? Is my will sick? Is it the dream in me that hampers all action? Days go by and sometimes I hear life going. And still nothing has happened yet, nothing real is around me yet."

Is it in the language itself that he must seek the tools of his art? Is it in some special study, closer knowledge of a subject? Or is it in a culture part inherited, part learned? But he is conscious of having to fight everything in his inheritance, while what he has achieved for himself is negligible; he is almost without education. His efforts at any given study were always broken off, partly because of the curious and surprising sense that he had to go back from an innate knowledge by laborious ways that finally, with much circumambulation, wound back to it. He needed books, but when in the Bibliothèque Nationale he found himself among those he had long coveted, everything in them seemed so important that he nearly succumbed to copying the whole text, and came away confused and full of superfluous information, his notes proving of little use to him afterward. "And I am similarly helpless in the face of those occurrences that come and go, without gift of choice, without composure of assimilation, a mirror turned this way and that out of which all the reflections fall . . . [T]hat is why I need so terribly to find the working material of my art. Somehow I must arrive at making things; not plastic, written things—realities, that emerge out of the handiwork." All the while he feels himself "awkward in life," losing precious moments. Hokusai, Leonardo, Rodin lived in their art and everything in them and their lives grew toward that only. "How shall one not be fearful who but seldom comes into his sanctuary, because out there where life is reared against him he catches himself in every trap and stubs himself blunt against every obstacle."

While this was his inner state of mind, he was nevertheless planning new work for the fall, in Italy. By the middle of August he was ready to move on once more, fond as he was of this moorland country, the stillness of its wide distances, the sweep and fullness of its winds. The house of his parents-in-law stood in a park at the back of which the Hamburg expresses passed, and their noise overriding that of the wind in the trees seemed, now that his thoughts were elsewhere, to disturb the quiet of his surroundings with a forewarning of travel and cities and new experiences to come. Now, at the wish of Rodin with whom she was studying, Clara was to spend a year in Rome and to a sojourn in the Eternal City Rilke was himself nothing loath. It would be his first visit. His deep interest in art had been intensified by the association with Rodin; and all the long background of such an artist's work had made him aware, beneath human history, of a more peaceful undercurrent in the history of the construction of "endless generations of things," and he was eager for fresh contact with the manifestations of antiquity. He theorized very beautifully upon what he was about to see, imagined himself a seeker of the "inner future in this past in which so much that is eternal was enclosed."

In the latter part of August 1903, then, he and his wife set out. They were to meet his parents in Marienbad. His father scarcely approved of the move: they lived so casually, was René really thoughtful of a secure future? nor of their vegetarianism; and as for their attire, fearing "abnormalities," he bids René order a suit from his Prague tailor and hopes that Clara will also be properly dressed. (René, at least in later years, was particular about his clothes: they were simple and they might be old, but they had an air of quality and comfort.) Thence they proceeded over Munich and Venice, in both of which cities Rilke particularly enjoyed the pictures of Zuloaga, whom they had met in Paris; and so over Florence to reach Rome a month later.

His disappointment of the first few days he expressed in many letters. Rome was "for the most part a bad museum," full of "senseless statues," lacked the expected Greek glories, had too many Renis and Guercinos—and he suffered much distress on observing the Italian talent for abusing animals. But gradually he found the valuable things, and he was able to throw off what troubled him about the city as he had not been able to do in Paris. The climate also, despite inclemencies, he felt to be less harmful. The Borghese gardens provided a refuge. And he speaks again and again of the fountains and the steps which were to him a constant source of refreshment and joy.

LETTER FIVE

He was now living at 5 via del Campidoglio, the last house (no longer standing) on a little terrace overlooking the Forum. The mood of Oberneuland was still upon him: he found it easier to collect himself sitting in the narrow circle of lamplight in his little room than out in the moonlight night, for which "one must first have become something again in order to feel it as space in which one is alone and in which one belongs." But he was not averse to his surroundings. A favorite walk he made every day included the ascent to the Capitol, "when, with the movement of one riding, the fine smooth bronze likeness of Marcus Aurelius mounts up stride by stride, from stair to stair." The little house he mentions, into which he was planning to move and where he hoped to "build a winter" for himself, was a former summerhouse—of one high-windowed room, with a flat roof from which one had a wide view of the Roman landscape—"the last and most remote in the large wild garden" of the Villa Strohl-Fern, adjoining the Borghese gardens. Here Clara was already installed in living quarters and a studio. "It is a happy circumstance that brought me to discover this place, and I think I shall take pleasure in it, in the evenings that may be spent there, in the great wide-open nights with the sound of animals that move, fruits that fall, winds that stir. . . . The most important thing to me will be to get to some sort of work there as soon as possible, the regular daily recurrence of which I may simply have to achieve by force if it does not want to come of its own accord. Then I shall go into the city comparatively seldom, often spend days on end out there and get my own little meals in my hermitage and be quite alone with my hands."

LETTER SIX

In the middle of November he moved in. But now he complained of prolonged rains, of inability to get to work, of waiting for the propitious hour, and how this waiting makes it always harder to begin, "and the happiness of being a beginner, which I hold to be the greatest, is small beside the fear of beginning." He wrote on December 19th: "I am now pretty well installed in the little house, it lacks nothing save that which I cannot give it—save life, which is in all things and in me; save work, which binds one thing to another and links everything with the great necessity; save joy, which comes from within and from activity; save patience, which can wait for what comes from afar."

Christmas brought the beginnings of "a sort of spring" after the long rains, but to Rilke and his wife its eve was to be "only a quiet hour, no more; we shall sit in the remote little garden house and think of those who are having Christmas; of our small dear Ruth and of ourselves, as though somewhere we were still the children we once were—the expectant, glad-timid Christmas children, upon whom great surprises descend like angels from within and without." It was not till the middle of January that one day, after a bit of "real work" sweeping the heavy pools of rainwater from his roof and clearing away the dried and fallen oak leaves, with the blood singing in him "as in a tree," he felt for the very first time after a long spell "a tiny little bit free and festive." He had now resumed after a considerable pause the translation of "The Song of the Host of Igor," an ancient Russian epic, and at this he was working every morning. Some reading, a book review or so—he did not want for occupation.

The good mood continued in February. He wrote to Ellen Key on the 6th: "It really seems as though things were quieting down around me, and even if my nerves, which are jumpy, sometimes dread disturbance from outside or uncertainty in health, there is yet much in me that is gathering itself together, and my longing to do something good, something really good, was never so great as now. I feel as though I had been sleeping for years or had been lying in the lowest hold of a ship that, loaded with heavy things, sailed through strange distances—— Oh to climb up on deck once more and feel the winds and the birds, and to see how the great, great nights come with their gleaming stars. . . ."

He had embarked upon "a sort of 2nd Part to the Stories-of-God book"; but by the middle of March (having also finished the Russian translation, which remains in manuscript) he was "stuck somewhere in the middle of it" and didn't know whether he would continue it or not.

LETTER SEVEN

Whatever its up and downs, this Roman winter proved an important one in his own growth. With his new work—whether he refers only to the second part of the *Stories*, or includes here the beginning of the *Notebooks*, which took place some time during this period—came the discovery that his way of working had changed, his powers of observation had grown more absorptive so that he would probably never again manage to write a book in ten days or evenings (as he had the *Stories of God*), but would spend a long time over each endeavor. "This is good," he wrote to Lou Andreas-Salomé on April 15th; "it marks progress toward that always-working which at any cost I must achieve for myself; perhaps a first step toward it. But in this change there lies a new danger too; to hold off outside disturbances for eight or ten days is possible—; but for weeks, for months? This fear pressed upon me, and is perhaps itself primarily to blame for the fact that my work wavered and with the beginning of March broke off. And what I took to be a little break and pause has become like heavy holidays hanging over me, that still continue. My progress is somehow rather like the steps of a convalescent, uncommonly weightless, tottering, and beyond all measure needing help. And the help is lacking."

By May he was already suffering from the heat, feeling good-for-nothing with headache, longing for more northerly realms, yet having no plan, no place to turn to. "Alas, that I have no parental country home, nowhere in the world a room with a few old things in it and a window looking out into great trees."

Yet his awareness of the alteration in himself had been leading him to a more positive attitude, a more practical sense of what he wanted to go after, of his own relation to life and work. The following, dated May 12th from Rome, and again to Lou Andreas-Salomé, marks a considerable change from the thoughts he had expressed to Ellen Key from Paris fifteen months earlier: "Art is a longest road through life, and when I think how slight and beginnerish what I have done till now is, I am not surprised that this production (which resembles a strip of half-tilled field a foot wide) does not sustain me. For plans bear no fruit, and seed prematurely sown does not sprout. But patience and work are real and can at any moment be transformed into bread. 'Il faut toujours travailler,' said Rodin whenever I attempted to complain to him about the schism in daily life; he knew no other solution, and this of course had been his. . . . To stick to my work and have every confidence in it, this I am learning from his great and greatly given example, as I learn patience from him; it is true, my experience tells me over and over that I haven't much strength to reckon with, for which reason I shall, so long as it is in any way possible, not do two things, not separate livelihood and work, rather try to find both in the one concentrated effort: only thus can my life become something good and necessary and heal together out of the tattered state for which heredity and immaturity have been responsible, into one bearing trunk.

"Therefore I shall determine my next place of abode, all else aside, from the point of view of work and that only. I want this the more, since I feel myself in the midst of developments and transitions (changes that affect observation and creation equally), which may slowly lead to that *toujours travailler* with which all outer and inner difficulties, dangers and confusions would really be in a certain sense overcome . . . for whoever can always work, can live too, must be able to."

He now had definite projects providing him with a variety of work. The first item he enumerates is the carrying on of the *Book of Hours*. The second is his new book, the *Notebooks*, "the close-knit prose of which is a schooling for me and an advance that had to be made so that I may be able later some day to write everything else—including the military novel." He seems to have been somewhat awed by this problem of writing prose, for four years later, in allusion to the same book, he expressed himself thus: "In writing poetry, one is always aided and even carried away by the rhythm of exterior things; for the lyric cadence is that of nature: of the waters, the wind, the night. But to write rhythmic prose one must go deep into oneself and find the anonymous and multiple rhythm of the blood. Prose needs to be built like a cathedral; there one is truly without a name, without ambition, without help: on scaffoldings, alone with one's consciousness." In addition to these two important works, he lists, further, an attempt at drama, and two monographs, one on Jacobsen, the other on Zuloaga. In connection with the latter, he planned to go to Spain, while for the sake of the former he was already studying Danish. Neither ever came to anything, nor, as we know, did the novel, which was apparently to have dealt with his Sankt-Pölten impressions.

That he realized the shortcomings of his own education has already been shown. "With my bringing up, conducted according to no plan, and with the intimidation from which I suffered in my growing years (everywhere encountering laughter and superiority, in my awkwardness repulsed by everyone), I never had a chance to learn much of the preparatory training, and most of the technicalities of living, which later are easy to everyone; my awareness is full to the brim with recollections of moments when all the people about me could do something and knew things and acted mechanically without thinking how to go about it, while I, embarrassed, didn't know where to begin, wasn't even able to imitate them by watching."

He now drew up, in addition to his writing plans, a list of studies for himself which implied no idle ambition. In order to carry them out he wanted to attend lectures in natural science and biology, to read and to see experiments; to learn to work with archives and historical documents "in so far as this is a technique and a handicraft"; to read the Grimm Brothers' Dictionary together with mediaeval literature; to go on with his Danish; to continue to read and translate Russian; to translate a book of Francis Jammes; and to read, among others, Michelet's studies in natural history, and his history of France; also the Goncourts' on the eighteenth century. He thought of going to one of the smaller German universities to have access to the necessary books and lectures.

The most significant thing about this list in the clue it gives us to the inner workings of his mind, is the interest in science, a new interest and based not so much on the desire to pursue any special branch of knowledge, any science as such, as on a craving for the knowable as a hold on life. He wrote—again to Lou Andreas-Salomé on May 12th—:

There are so many things about which some old man ought to tell one while one is little; for when one is grown one would know them as a matter of course. There are the starry skies, and I do not know what mankind has already learned about them, not even the order of the stars do I know. And so it is with flowers, with animals, with the simplest laws, that function here and there and go through the world in a few strides from beginning to

end. How life occurs, how it operates in ordinary ani-
mals, how it ramifies and spreads, how life blossoms,
how it bears: all that I long to learn. Through participa-
tion in it all to bind myself more firmly to reality—which
so often denies me—to be of it, not only in feeling but
also by knowledge, always and always; that I believe is
what I need, to become more sure and not so homeless.
You sense that I do not want sciences; for each one requires
a lifetime and no life is long enough to master even its
beginnings; but I want to cease to be an exile, one who
cannot read the deeper record of his time that points far-
ther forward and reaches farther back, a prisoner who
senses everything but has not the small certainty whether
just now it is day or evening, spring or winter. I should
like somewhere, where that can be done, to learn that
which I should probably know if I had been allowed to
grow up in the country and among more vital people,
and that which an impersonal and hasty school failed
to tell me, and whatever else has since been found and
recognized and belongs to it. Not art history and other
histories, not the nature of philosophic systems do I want
to learn—I want to be allowed to acquire, to achieve only
a few great and simple certainties, that are there for all:
I want to be allowed to ask a few questions, questions
such as children ask, irrelevant to the outsider but full of
a family likeness for me who know their birth and descent
unto the tenth generation.

He hoped in this way to gain a more certain grasp of any work he might undertake, to have resources that would always stand him in good stead; and to save himself from that "daily evidence of my inefficiency, of that being excluded, which life makes me feel again and again, whenever I try to draw near it at any point."

At this time he was still so acutely aware of not yet having done anything important, anything demonstrable, that, although he very well recognized the necessity of earning where he could and the privilege of being sponsored by so fine a person, he looked "(in confidence) with terror" upon the efforts of his good friend Ellen Key to attract attention to his work. He feared that in her earnestness and enthusiasm, in confusing her knowledge of him through his letters with that which she had drawn from what she knew of his poems, she would make unjustified claims and give an impression of finality to his expression of ideas which his so-far-published works did not possess. "And over and above all this I feel: if anyone needs seclusion, it is I."

LETTER EIGHT

These efforts of Ellen Key, however, brought him some "sympathetic invitations in the North" and one of these he promptly accepted, traveling, when he finally left Rome in the month of June, 1904, to Sweden via Copenhagen. Borgeby gård, Flädie, was a great farming estate in the southern province of Skåne. Rilke had soon found out the whole long history of the old castle, a tower of which had been rebuilt into living quarters; he enjoyed the gardens and the orchards and ate with pleasure and benefit their vegetables, fruits and berries, served at a well-set table; he loved the fields and the peace of pasturing creatures ("we have 200 cows," he wrote on the night of his arrival), the horses, oxen, dogs; found entertainment in the weak-jointed endeavors of a new foal to get about, and the learning of young storks to clapper; took delight in the great trees of the park and the long well-kept chestnut-bordered driveways, in the winds and the storms as they passed over this fertile land. His letters are full of feeling for the productive life about him and reflect a contentment of spirit that goes with it; it was one of the most tranquil episodes of his life. No wonder he spent the whole summer here. He was not creatively occupied: "Summer was never my high time." But he read and wrote letters, taught himself Danish largely by reading Jacobsen and Herman Bang and translating Sören Kierkegaard's letters to his fiancée, made acquaintance with Scandinavian literature generally, while inwardly he felt himself building, preparing something invisible but fundamental. He deliberately thought it best to look upon this time really as one of recreation and live it accordingly, although the old sense of not having achieved what he was bound to do sometimes creeps through: "I miss the gladness, miss something or other that I should have previously done. A point of departure, some evidence, the passing of a test in my own eyes."

He wrote to Clara on the evening of July 27th:

> . . . *Thanks for Kappus' letter. He has a hard time. And this is only the beginning. And he is right about it: in childhood we have used up too much strength, too much grown-people's strength,—that may be true for a whole generation. Or true over and over again for individuals. What shall one say about it? That life has unending possibilities of renewal. Yes, but this too: that the using of strength in a certain sense is always increase of strength also; for fundamentally we have to do only with a wide cycle: all strength that we give away comes over us again, experienced and altered. Thus it is in prayer. And what is there, truly done, that is not prayer?*
>
> *And another thing, with regard to the recreation idea. There are here, amid this realm of fields, spots of dark ploughed land. They are empty, and yet lie they here as though the bright culms round about them were there for their sakes, rows of fencing for their protection. I asked what was doing with these dark acres. They told me: c'est de la terre en repos. So lovely, you see, can rest be, and so it looks alongside work. Not disquieting, but so that one gathers a deep confidence and the feel of a big time. . . .*

LETTER NINE

When after this prolonged sojourn he went in the autumn to visit other friends of Ellen Key in their country house near Göteborg, he had still not settled to anything that in his own eyes amounted to a specific piece of work. This does not mean that he was ever idle. He continually worked, writing letters, articles, book reviews, always following to some extent the outlines of study he had made for himself. Two visits to the Samskola, a modern community school for boys and girls, made such an impression upon him that he wrote an essay on it which he was later asked to read at the school and which had a wide influence when it was soon afterward published. He cared enough about it to consider whether he and his wife could not start something of the sort in North Germany, but doubted whether they were the right people to do it "with our small strength which should not be divided. And I with my great ignorance and never having learned anything! . . . But it was good for us to see the Samskola; an encouragement goes forth from it in far-reaching waves as from a fine, happy future that is sure." During November he finished the *Weisse Fürstin* in its final form.

He still fostered the idea of studying somewhere: "Since I cannot arrive from within at the solution for work, it will probably have to come from without." He needs to open up his work to new tributaries; not that he lacks experiencing and living but he has not the power to arrange, coördinate: must learn to seize and hold, must learn to work. The not having achieved this bothers him like a bad conscience. Still, he senses an advance and hopes that he can now make certain resolves to lead a more industrious and conscious life than heretofore.

This state of mind remains characteristic of him for some time to come, with the fluctuations inevitable to such a temperament, such a physique. For the next four years, which concern this chronicle only because at their expiration he once more communicated with the Young Poet, Rilke moved about without any fixed abode, much as we have seen him do within the time discussed and as he was to do for most of his life. This condition of affairs often oppressed him: "It costs so much effort and good will and imagination to set up anywhere an appearance of four walls out of the contents of a few trunks, and I would like so much to use what I have of such equipment directly for work, not on the preparation for it." Oberneuland and Worpswede, Capri, Berlin, visits to friends in various parts of Germany; lecture tours including Dresden and Prague, Vienna and even Venice; and for the most part Paris. He takes a growing interest in Cézanne; he is in touch with Hammershøi, Bojer, Verhaeren, von Hofmannsthal, Stefan Zweig; meets Bernard Shaw, who comes to pose for Rodin; sees something of Zuloaga and Bourdelle. Meanwhile he has been adding poems to the *Buch der Bilder* for its second edition. In October 1907 the essay on Rodin appears; a new volume of verse, *Neue Gedichte* (*New Poems*), about the same time. He is now more closely thrown with Rodin, even living in a little stone house in the garden at Meudon and acting as "a sort of secretary."

The value of Rodin's example for Rilke lay, as we have seen before, in its showing him the possibility of taking hold, of persisting, in bringing him finally to realize that he must and could do the same in his own way, making him eager to get at his own labors again. The very dominance of the personality which as a living precept taught him this, made him restive, full of desire for a year or two of hard work by himself. For behind all his hesitations and delays there was the persevering will that held him to his purpose. In May 1906 a misunderstanding over some small matter of Rodin's correspondence caused a break in their relations, which, however, was healed again in November 1907. It greatly distressed Rilke, but in the light of his own development it fell perhaps as a fortunate coincidence. Aware of the irritability of the aging artist, who had not been well just then, he took a large view of it from the start, and it did not injure the roots of the profound influence Rodin's way of working and of living had had upon him.

LETTER TEN

To Rodin, "mon cher et seul Ami," Rilke wrote on December 29th: "I am able more and more to make use of that long patience you have taught me by your tenacious example; that patience which, disproportionate to ordinary life which seems to bid us haste, puts us in touch with all that surpasses us."

He is making good use of that patience. His task is the writing of *The Notebooks of Malte Laurids Brigge*, "that difficult, difficult book" which, despite the intense effort and the mental anguish it has cost him, he is now bringing through. It is a good moment at which to leave him, calmer, more content, because he is working.

M. D. HERTER NORTON

AFTERWORD

Along a prominent corridor at Norton's New York office there is a row of portraits of chairmen and presidents past, beginning with William Warder Norton. One portrait is unlike the others—that of M. D. H. Norton, known to family and friends as Polly, and during her lifetime known to staff, with suitable decorousness, as Mrs. Norton. Mrs. Norton never had those vaunted job titles or official roles, and so her portrait (see page vi) was not part of that corridor gallery until 2007, decades too late. Until that time, the company's origin story firmly placed her on the sidelines.

The reasons for this state of things are old news, especially to women, but when I joined Norton as a college traveler—or sales rep—in 1983 the old news was changing. That was the year we launched the groundbreaking *Norton Anthology of Literature by Women* (1985). Because of that book I saw firsthand—and perhaps played a part in helping English professors in my midwestern territory see—how the recovery of neglected writers whose works open a new way of reading the literary past can change the story for generations of readers. In the canon wars that raged during my first two decades at Norton I saw one unequivocal win: a broad acknowledgment, first in the academy but eventually embraced by general readers, that old narratives need reframing. This reconsideration of the stories we tell was a wake-up call to bring campus lessons back to 500 Fifth Avenue—to revise our various narratives "About Norton," to rehang the portrait wall to make room for Polly's photograph, and, most important, year after year, to tell newly hired Norton colleagues a different origin story, one that made clear that Warder and Polly Norton co-founded W. W. Norton & Company.

Reframing requires materials, and when telling stories, those materials come ideally in the form of primary documents. Fortunately, Mrs. Norton gave the company its most influential and enduring document: the Joint Shareholders Agreement. Widowed suddenly in 1945, it was Mrs. Norton who made possible the vision it formalizes, that is, to enable the company to continue thriving as an independent publisher beyond the Nortons' active presence. As the agreement states, "It is the desire of the parties hereto that the publishing ideals and policies on which the business of the Company was founded and in accordance with which it has been conducted, shall be maintained and fostered." Fully executed in 1952, the Joint Shareholders Agreement put the ownership of the firm in the hands of its senior leadership and opened the door to employee ownership. Turning the company over to its staff was then, and more than seventy years later remains, an extraordinary business move and a bold vote of trust in leadership that understands the organization in a sustained and nuanced way, and in the durability of the vision that she and Warder brought to their shared life's work.

The M. D. H. Norton translation of Rilke's *Letters to a Young Poet* (1934) plays a key role in my reframing project, for it contains the translator's rich and, to my ear, self-revealing "Chronicle, 1903–1908," in which she briefly comments on Rilke's life circumstances and imagines his challenges and insights as an artist. Damion Searls is right to note (in his foreword to this edition) that the signature quality of M. D. H. Norton's translation is its "stately grandeur," employed in service of her sense of Rilke as "the canonical Great Man, one who speaks to us all." But what I see in her Chronicle is empathy that moves beyond judgments of greatness and acknowledges the everyday effort of Rilke's life as an artist. She is both generous and practical, and she writes, I think, with the fellow feeling of the serious artist she was, asserting that only creative activity gives the artist "that utmost satisfaction which both elates and calms, both inspires and exhausts." But to my publisher's ear, most significant is her notion that readers—who are typically not artists—might search for inspiration in the arts and sciences "based not so much on the desire to pursue any special branch of knowledge, any science as such, as on a craving for the knowable as a hold on life." "The knowable as a hold on life" is a striking, even musical phrase. It is especially resonant to me, echoing as it does the Nortons' description of their first publishing foray, that is, the publication as pamphlets of free lectures delivered at Cooper Union by leading scholars who would "bring to the public the knowledge of our time." This idea is the tie that binds those first pamphlets to the firm's sustained commitment over a century to serious nonfiction and its powerful presence in educational publishing.

To color in the origin of Polly Norton's passion for "the knowable," I've turned to secondary sources, and taken one leap of imagination. Her parents, Christian and Susan Herter, were exceptional role models, both as individuals and as partners. Trained as a medical doctor, Christian Herter also focused on research, building a laboratory on the top floor of the family home at 919 Madison Avenue, where Susan Herter saw to the finances of staffing and equipping the lab. The Herter lab was instrumental in creating the field of biochemistry, and Christian Herter advanced that new field through teaching at Columbia University and co-founding and financing the *Journal of Biological Chemistry*. While the

Herters raised their family in a setting of great privilege in Gilded Age Manhattan, they did so with an intense, unorthodox focus on a home education open to new people and ideas. One appreciator of Christian Herter writes that "Herter's social world . . . allowed him latitude to cultivate—in areas of politics, religion, morality, and certain social thinking—an outlook that would be branded as heresy." Here is my leap: the Herters had five children, but only their three daughters survived to adulthood. I can imagine that the tragic loss of their two sons in infancy may have turned Christian and Susan Herter's minds in heretical ways to the education of their daughters. Polly was introduced to science in childhood, over lunch with her family and her father's staff—chemists, bacteriologists, and physicians working in the top-floor lab, where as a teenager she joined them as lab assistant. Underpinned by Christian's hypothesis that "until girls and women generally have opportunities more on a parity with boys and men in respect to education, it will be impossible to estimate justly the degree of the assumed disparity between men and women," the Herters' program of private education prepared Polly, Christine, and Susan Herter for lives alert to "the knowable" and its potential for civic good.

As large a role as science played in Polly's early years, her humanistic accomplishments most define her. A student of

The Herter family playing music in their drawing room, ca. 1911.
From left to right: Susan Herter, Susan Dows Herter Dakin,
Mary Dows Herter (Polly), Christine Herter Kendall.
PHOTO PROVIDED BY AND REPUBLISHED WITH
PERMISSION OF ALEXIA NORTON JONES

Polly Norton served with the auxiliary Red Cross
in Paris in 1917, when she was twenty-three years old.
PHOTO COURTESY OF JACK RIZZITELLO AND REPRINTED
WITH PERMISSION FROM ALEXIA NORTON JONES

the violin from childhood, at age eleven she spent a year in Frankfurt studying viola and learning German. Returning to Manhattan, she attended the Institute of Musical Art—now called Juilliard—and organized and played in a string quartet that regularly performed publicly. Her first book, *String Quartet Playing*, was published in 1925 by Carl Fischer Music. "Of unusual intellectual and scholarly attainment" is how Polly's younger sister Susan described her, as a prelude to this memorable passage: "In 1921, Mary Herter married Wm. Warder Norton, a businessman of small means, who has gone with success into the publishing business. . . . Mrs. Norton, a writer of ability, has given up her professional career as a musician and has become a strong factor in the success of her husband's business."[*]

That Victorian-sounding finish was not the last word— "*Reader, I married him.*" It was arguably the first word, for Polly and Warder together were the "strong factor" in the company's success. Each put up $2,500 to launch the People's Institute Publishing Company, as the company was first named. Together they edited transcripts of the lectures given at Cooper Union, and assembled the printed lectures into boxed sets on their dining room table. Together Warder and Polly built Norton's lists in psychology, publishing H. A. Overstreet, Karen Horney,

---

[*] Susan's quote about her sister comes from an unpublished family history. This source, as well as many other valuable documents about Polly, was provided by Alexia Norton Jones.

Otto Fenichel, John Watson, Freud's *Introductory Lectures*; and in philosophy, notably works by Bertrand Russell and José Ortega y Gasset. Polly was the driving force behind the fledgling music list, co-translating Norton's first music book, *The Story of Music* (1927), and bringing eminent musicologists Gustave Reese, Paul Henry Lang, and Curt Sachs to Norton. In the thirties and forties, she translated and published nine volumes of poems and letters by Rainer Maria Rilke, making Rilke's work available to American readers for the first time. Yes, she was a strong factor.

And yet, with a hundred years of hindsight, I wonder sometimes whether the gifted violinist who gave up her career as a professional musician would have seen herself as burdened with "the problem that has no name," explosively laid bare by Betty Friedan in *The Feminine Mystique* (Norton, 1964); or whether Adrienne Rich's "Diving into the Wreck" (Norton, 1973) would have touched a nerve, with its evocation of names gone missing:

> We are, I am, you are
> by cowardice or courage
> the ones who find our way
> back to this scene
> carrying a knife, a camera
> a book of myths
> in which
> our names do not appear.

I am certain Polly would be proud to have published authors whose work profoundly altered readers' grasp of "the knowable as a hold on life." With a hundred years of hindsight, I in turn am proud knowing what Warder and Polly Norton themselves achieved, and then wondrously put in the care of generations of like-minded, language- and idea-loving "Nortonians." Looking ahead, I feel deep optimism in what the next hundred years hold for the independent and employee-owned publishing firm the Nortons co-founded.

JULIA A. REIDHEAD
Chairman and President
W. W. Norton & Company